University college of North Wales

British universities

Notes and summaries contributed to the Welsh university discussion

University college of North Wales

British universities
Notes and summaries contributed to the Welsh university discussion

ISBN/EAN: 9783337154578

Printed in Europe, USA, Canada, Australia, Japan

Cover: Foto ©Paul-Georg Meister /pixelio.de

More available books at **www.hansebooks.com**

BRITISH UNIVERSITIES:

NOTES AND SUMMARIES CONTRIBUTED TO THE WELSH UNIVERSITY DISCUSSION BY MEMBERS OF THE SENATE OF THE UNIVERSITY COLLEGE OF NORTH WALES.

WITH A GENERAL INTRODUCTION

BY

W. RHYS ROBERTS, M.A.,

PROFESSOR OF GREEK IN THE UNIVERSITY COLLEGE OF NORTH WALES, BANGOR; LATE FELLOW OF KING'S COLLEGE, CAMBRIDGE.

Coder safon dysgeidiaeth yn uwch yng ngolwg y wlad. — Dr. Lewis Edwards.

J. E. CORNISH,
St. Ann's Square, Manchester.
—
1892.

CONTENTS.

	PAGE
GENERAL INTRODUCTION	3

British Universities.

ENGLAND:—

- I. OXFORD. H. R. Reichel - - - - - - - - 32
- II. CAMBRIDGE. E. V. Arnold - - - - - - - - 45
- III. DURHAM. E. V. Arnold - - - - - - - - 50
- IV. LONDON:—
  - (a) University of London. R. W. Phillips - - - 51
  - (b) Proposed Albert University. G. B. Mathews - 55
- V. VICTORIA. W. Rhys Roberts - - - - - - - 57

SCOTLAND:—

- I. EDINBURGH. J. J. Dobbie - - - - - - - - 65
- II. ABERDEEN. [Reference to preceding Summary] - - 77
- III. GLASGOW. Andrew Gray - - - - - - - - 77
- IV. ST. ANDREWS. Andrew Gray - - - - - - - 82

IRELAND:—

- I. UNIVERSITY OF DUBLIN. H. R. Reichel - - - - 85
- II. (a) QUEEN'S UNIVERSITY
  (b) ROYAL UNIVERSITY OF IRELAND } H. R. Reichel 86

GENERAL INTRODUCTION

These Notes and Summaries have been prepared, at somewhat short notice, by a few College teachers who, feeling a sincere interest in the future of higher education in Wales, feel also how deeply that future will be influenced, for good or for evil, by the character of the proposed Welsh University. One great want of the moment is (so the writers venture to think) fuller information as to the machinery usually employed in university administration; and in order to help in meeting this want, they have made brief analyses of the constitution and regulations of the existing universities which lie nearest to hand—those of Great Britain and Ireland.

Universities have had a long history. It is a vast tract of time that separates the University of Athens (Greece), which was in full existence long before the birth of Christ, from the University opened at Athens (Georgia) in the early years of the present century. And no less vast is the difference in character between institutions described by the common name of University; for the proud title has too often been rashly invoked. The experience of the past is, however, always valuable, whether it has to tell of a vaulting ambition which o'erleaps itself, or of high ideals and of means skilfully adapted to ends.

As has just been implied, the earliest of all universities was that of Athens. The name itself, it is true, came later; but the teachers not only of Athens, but of Alexandria, made their cities what we can only describe as university centres for the then known world. The schools of Athens were philosophical chiefly; the studies pursued in the Museum of Alexandria were mainly 'scientific,' if we may use the word, as in matters academical one would like to see it used, of method rather than of matter. The Library at Alexandria is said to have contained 700,000 volumes; the Museum was a noble college, with provision for Resident Fellows. Owing to this liberal endowment of research by the Ptolemies, and owing also to the more serious spirit in which knowledge was pursued in the Egyptian capital, Alexandria soon surpassed its older rival in solid achievement, though the glamour of Athens—the fascination of her history, literature, and art—kept her schools prominent till as late a date as 529 A.D., when the Emperor Justinian closed them, and withdrew the state subventions granted under the Antonines. The scholars of Alexandria had, during the second and third centuries before Christ, done some really enduring work, in grammar and criticism on the one hand, and in physical science on the other. The grammarians collected, purified, and preserved for future ages, the works of the great Greek writers. The chief of these grammarians was Aristarchus, the Homeric critic, who was sometimes called the 'diviner,' from his surpassing skill in divining the readings and meanings of the authors edited by him. In science, the great names were Eratosthenes, the geographer (who was also a grammarian, philosopher, and mathematician, and a man of real learning, not a mere sciolist), Archimedes of Syracuse, the mathematician and inventor, Hipparchus, the father of astronomy, and Eucleides ('Euclid'), the author of the 'Elements.' Institutions which aided, if they did not produce, men such as these, more than justified the liberality of their founders.

The organisation by successive emperors of higher education at Rome, Constantinople, and various provincial centres, needs but a passing mention. The measures taken were, generally speaking, the outcome of statecraft rather than of a genuine interest in learning, and the results were consequently meagre.

The Romano-Hellenic schools declined as Christianity advanced. Owing to the prevailing distrust of secular learning, the Christian schools themselves made little, if any, progress from the sixth to the eighth century. In the ninth century Charlemagne made a determined effort to inaugurate a new era in ecclesiastical education. His aims, being far in advance of his time, were only imperfectly realised; but the great schools which he established at Paris, Pavia, and Bologna, may fairly be considered as the precursors of the Universities which grew up later in those cities.

The *Schola Salernitana*, a medical school which arose at Salernum, near Naples, as early as the ninth century, was hardly a university, though the position has sometimes been claimed for it. The earliest of the mediæval universities were, rather, those of Paris and Bologna, which received their charters—charters of confirmation rather than of establishment—in the twelfth century. They were not the direct creation of church or state, but sprang up of themselves, reflecting the zeal of enthusiastic teachers who gathered students round them, and the common desire of teachers and taught to promote and guard the interests of learning by means of associations similar to the trade-guilds established in the interests of commerce. The earliest universities to be deliberately founded were those of Prague and Vienna. Law studies, developed and made attractive by Irnerius, prevailed at Bologna; Arts (mainly theological) studies at Paris. Bologna was more of a professional school than Paris, and the fact that the latter university pursued knowledge more entirely for its own sake added greatly to its subsequent influence. At the beginning of the thirteenth century there were (it is said) 10,000 students at Bologna, in the time of Roger Bacon 20,000; while the attendance at Paris was as large, or even larger. And though such statements savour of mediæval exaggeration, yet the actual number was undoubtedly extremely large. Most of the students came from distant places; and hence, both at Bologna and at Paris, those who were from the same country or district found it convenient to group themselves in the self-governing societies termed 'nations.' At Paris there was, for example, an 'English Nation,' which, in the reign of Henry III. migrated, in a body, to Oxford and Cambridge, owing to fatal encounters between the municipal and university authorities. Oxford and Cambridge (as well as Bologna and Paris) may be regarded as having commenced their university existence somewhere in the twelfth century.

Two important points to note with regard to all these universities are: (1) They were lay, and not monastic, in character, and owed much of their vigour and vitality to this absence of restriction to a single class. It is true that they were, to some extent, subject to Papal authority, but only (they liked to feel) as to a final court of appeal. Each university looked upon itself as being (to adopt a designation still employed by Cambridge) a 'literary republic.' (2) Their name of *university* did not refer to any universality in the curriculum of study, but to the fact that teachers and taught formed in them a corporation (the *universitas magistrorum et scholarium*). The equivalent term *studium generale* similarly meant 'a place of study open to all,' that is to say, not confined to students who were under monastic discipline.

In 1348 was founded, by Charles IV. of Bohemia, the University of Prague. Through a secession in 1409, Prague lost its German teachers and students, who repaired to Vienna, Erfurt, Heidelberg, and Leipzig. They thus strengthened the German universities, the constitution of which was closely modelled upon that of Prague. It will be seen, upon referring to the *Table of Dates* given later, that three of the four Scottish universities were also founded in this, the fifteenth, century. The University of Leyden, it is interesting to note, was created, in the latter part of the sixteenth century, by no King or Pope, but by the Dutch Republic, which thus rewarded the people of Leyden for their gallant defence of the town against the Spaniards. It is not necessary, in a rapid sketch, to particularise other universities. How great the stir among them all was during the period of the Revival of Learning will best be realized by one who has carefully followed the career of some single mediæval scholar, Erasmus let us say, and seen him at Paris, at Oxford (consorting there with Linacre, Grocyn, and Colet), at Louvain, and at Cambridge, not to mention many other university towns of lesser note to which he paid flying or protracted visits.

After the period of the Reformation, the universities of Germany lost their youthful vigour, and declined. But for that falling-off they have since made ample amends. The revival may be said to have begun with the foundation of Halle (1693) and Göttingen

(1736), and to have reached its culmination in the striking growth of the three great universities of Berlin, Bonn, and Munich, all of which have been established since the commencement of the present century. It has been observed by Mr. Mullinger that "a notable characteristic in the University of Berlin at the time of its foundation was its entire repudiation of attachment to any particular creed or school of thought, and professed subservience only to the interests of science and learning."

To-day, as we all know, there is no university system which equals that of Germany in the magnitude of its results. There are no abodes of learning like those of Germany, none where the workers are so unwearied, so successful, or so numerous. The specialist cannot read over the list of professors, past and present, in the German universities, without meeting the names of men whose works mark advances, great or small, in his particular branch of study; nor will the man of more general culture look in vain for some of the still more distinguished few whose achievements have commanded the attention of all who (without special knowledge of their own) are interested in the wider aspects of the mental movements of the day.

What, it may be well to ask, are the broad outlines of the system under which the latent capacity of the German has been thus signally developed, and under which learning has become a national rather than an individual characteristic?

First of all, it must of course not escape notice that this system is but *a part of a larger whole;* and it should be added that this larger whole was designed early in this century by men like Wilhelm von Humboldt, F. A. Wolf, and Schleiermacher, who were patriots and saw that their country, then humbled by Napoleon, needed quickening on the intellectual side, and who were also marked out by ability and attainment for the task which they took in hand. The reforms then introduced affected the whole range of education. They cannot be treated of here, but it is impossible to overrate the indebtedness of the German

Universities to the schools which feed them. These schools are manned by teachers whose qualifications are most rigorously tested both during and after their university course; and the students sent to the universities must (if their residence is to be officially recognised) previously pass a Leaving Examination—the *Abiturientenexamen.* The purpose of this Leaving Examination is to ascertain whether the preliminary general training is complete, so that the candidate may with advantage now enter upon a more special line of study. The Germans are firm believers in a systematic training. Before a candidate can qualify for state and professional appointments he must go through a regular school and university course : no mere examinations are allowed to take the place of this indispensable preliminary.

The second point to be noticed is the number and distribution of the German universities and the attendance at them. A glance at them from this point of view will at once show their truly *national and popular character.* They are twenty-one in all. If we follow the map of Germany from west to east and work down from north to south, we shall find that they run thus : Kiel, Rostock, Greifswald, Königsberg, Münster, Berlin, Göttingen, Halle, Leipzig, Breslau, Bonn, Marburg, Jena, Giessen, Würzburg, Heidelberg, Erlangen, Strassburg, Tübingen, Freiburg, Munich. In the number of students attending them they rank as follows, to begin with the largest and end with the smallest : Berlin, 5,527 ; Munich, 3,551 ; Leipzig, 3,458 ; Halle, 1,584 ; Würzburg, 1,544 ; Tübingen, 1,393 ; Bonn, 1,386 ; Breslau, 1,246 ; Freiburg, 1,230 ; Heidelberg, 1,171 ; Erlangen, 1,054 ; Marburg, 952 ; Strassburg, 947 ; Göttingen, 890 ; Greifswald, 832 ; Königsberg, 682 ; Jena, 675 : Giessen, 549 ; Kiel, 489 ; Münster, 385 ; Rostock, 371.

The proportion of university students to the population in England and Germany respectively was estimated a few years ago as follows :—The population of Germany was, in round numbers, 45,000,000; that of England and Wales, 26,000,000. The number of students in the German universities was 24,187 ; in the English universities in which residence is required, viz., Oxford,

Cambridge, Durham, and Victoria, it was less than 5,500. That is to say, the population of Germany was less than double that of England, but its students were more than four times as numerous as those attending the English universities. Or, to put it in another way, in Germany there was one university student for every 1,860 inhabitants; in England, one university student for every 4,730 inhabitants. It is, however, to be borne in mind that in Germany the universities are the avenues to the professions universally, and not, as in England, occasionally and accidentally. A satisfactory university career is one of the qualifications required by Government, not merely of the future schoolmaster or minister of religion, but also of the future doctor or lawyer.

A further point, and one of primary importance, is the *finance* of the German universities. The fees must be low to admit of such an astonishing number of students. What proportion do these fees form of the total income of the universities? How is the deficiency made up? And how, in particular, is that magnificent provision made for the endowment of research? The answer is simple. In Germany, poor though the country is when compared with England, the bulk of the cost of education is defrayed by means of annual taxation. In the case of university expenditure in particular, the percentage contributed in students' fees has been estimated at 9·3, the contribution of the State at 72; the balance coming from endowments and other sources. During the last fifty years the number of students attending the German universities has increased greatly, but the state has not taken advantage of this increase, either to raise the fees, or to keep the supply of teachers, and therewith the outlay, stationary. On the contrary, the proportion of teachers to students is as high as 1 to 11—almost three times as high as in the Scottish universities, where the proportion is (or was till recently) 1 : 30. The liberal attitude of the German state towards teaching and research has been forcibly described by Mr. Bryce: "The State expends on the German universities nearly eight times as much as they receive from students' fees, and deems the money well spent. She is liberal in the provision of apparatus. She encourages, by payment, the semi-professorial class of *Privatdocenten*. She maintains chairs in subjects for which few students can be expected. She recognizes, by allowing some leisure for, and by the distribution of promotion, the function of the professor in advancing the frontiers of science by independent inquiry, inquiry which, though it tends indirectly to improve his teaching, often runs into fields where few students can follow." Referring more particularly to the increase of the professorial staffs, Mr. Bryce says, "it has taken place partly by adding on fresh teachers for the old subjects, such as Latin and Greek, but still more by founding new chairs for new subjects, such as Oriental and Romance languages, geography, archæology, and by subdividing departments, which have been recently developed, such as those connected with political economy, political science, physiology, and biology." It need not be pointed out how much this liberal provision of teaching means, both to the advanced student who requires individual assistance, and to the professor himself, who has thus some time at his disposal for the prosecution of original research. It is here, in this band of men of learning and science who are for ever extending the bounds of knowledge, that we have the really characteristic feature of the German system, and that which has made the German universities famous. That there should be over 1,800 professors and other university teachers at work in Germany, and that each one has, on an average, only 11[*] students, is certainly a fact to be well pondered here in Britain.

The last point for consideration in connexion with the German universities is their *constitution and general working*. Naturally only the broad outlines of the main features of the system can here be given.

The first thing which strikes one is the simplicity of the machinery as compared with that of the British universities. This is partly due to the fact that in Germany the administration of university education, as well as of education generally, is in the hands of a separate State Department.

[*] Nine, or less, in Arts and Science subjects.

The Minister of Education is the ultimate authority in the government of the German Universities. He appoints the professors, and it is to him and parliament that the university authorities must submit any important changes they intend to make. He has in each university a representative, called a *Curator*, who sees to it that the state regulations are observed.

But practically the university authorities are in Germany allowed a very free hand. Even in the case of professorial appointments they have the right of proposing names to the Minister. The university authorities are as follows: (1) The *Rector*, who is elected by the full professors, and (2) the *Academical Senate*, which is elected by the full professors, and consists of the rector, his predecessor in office, and either the whole, or a considerable number, of the full professors in each faculty. The academical senate regulates the internal affairs of the university.

The faculties are usually four in number, viz., theology, law, medicine, and philosophy. 'Philosophy' has a wide acceptation, and includes languages and literatures on the one hand, and the mathematical and natural sciences on the other. Each faculty consists of the full professors in it, presided over by a dean elected by themselves. The chief function of a faculty is to arrange that complete and systematic instruction shall be given in the department of study under its charge. Its curricula are published after consultation with all the teachers concerned.

The full professors and the assistant professors are alike appointed by the state. The state—the parsimonious German state—further reserves to itself the right, and sometimes exercises it, of appointing at the regular salary a distinguished man as additional full professor in a faculty in which there are no vacancies. The income of the full professorships, which—for Germany—is large, consists of a fixed stipend and of the fees paid at lectures other than those (at least two a week) which the professor is required to deliver free of charge. The full professors are usually chosen from among the assistant professors (or 'extraordinary' professors), and the assistant professors from the class of the *Privatdocenten*.

This class of *Privatdocenten* forms a notable feature in

the German system. Here we have the great recruiting-ground and training-ground for the highest teaching posts in the universities. The position of a *Privatdocent* is semi-official and honourable; it is not, like that of our Private Tutors, irresponsible and commercial. After distinguishing himself as a student, the would-be *Privatdocent* receives, if he satisfies certain tests, his appointment from the Faculty in connexion with which he proposes to work. If any stipend at all is paid him, it is only a small one; he is dependent almost entirely upon the proceeds of his lectures. But those lectures are given in the university classrooms, and form a part of the recognized university system. Thus there opens out a fine field for distinction, not to speak of the absolute necessity of exertion. The rivalry (for it may become that) between the professors and the *Privatdocenten* is generally a friendly one, and re-acts beneficially on both. The number of *Privatdocenten* is usually as large as that of the assistant professors, and about half that of the full professors.

Here, as elsewhere, we see how much Germany owes in educational matters to the existence of a *system*. In other countries the same amount of money might be spent, but the professors (to whom, let it be repeated, the real reputation of the German Universities is due) might disappoint expectation. But in Germany you have as safeguards for getting the right man as professor, and keeping him right, such points in the system as these :— Long training and adequate testing at school and at the university, close contact with teachers who are themselves working and advancing knowledge by means of systematic study, an opportunity of showing gifts of teaching and investigation as *Privatdocent*, appointment as professor by a high-placed officer of State, the tenure of an office held honourable by the nation and with a status and traditions and governing powers of its own, the prospect of further promotion over a wide field, the stimulus of excellent students and colleagues, the feeling of connexion with a great corporation which is supplied with all the appliances of learning, and is surrounded by a true atmosphere of learning. With such an organised system, it is not likely that a man will either mistake his vocation to begin with, or when he adopts it will prove unworthy of it.

A few words may be added, from the student's point of view, with regard to residence, lecture-fees, degree-examinations, etc. The normal university course is three years; in medicine, four or five. Residence is required for degrees, but students are not obliged to spend all their time in the same university. The class-fees vary from 16s. to £1. 14s. for the *Semester*, or half-session. Considerable freedom is allowed with regard to choice of lectures, but regular attendance upon those chosen is expected. The degree of doctor is conferred as the result of a written dissertation (to which great importance is attached), an oral examination, and a sufficient attendance at university lectures. The degree varies in value at different universities, and the examination for it is not so searching as the *Staatsprüfung* which has to be undergone by the future lawyer, doctor, clergyman, schoolmaster, or civil servant, and which (in one shape or another) is looked forward to by the great majority of university students, who alone are admissible to it.

One obvious conclusion to draw from German experience is that, in constituting any new university, ample provision should be made from the start for attaching to it, as far as possible, its most promising graduates. This cannot be done in this country by simply allowing those graduates to teach and take the fees; students are too few and the cost of living is too high. University Fellowships or Scholarships will be required in addition. In connexion with this and other points, it will be well to see what the American universities, the best of which gladly learn from those of Germany, have to teach us.

It is not easy to say a word in general about the chartered universities of America: they are too numerous and too various. Some, like Harvard and Yale, can hold their heads high among the oldest in Europe; while others (more than two hundred in all, according to the estimate of a most unprejudiced and competent observer) would be more respected if they resigned their position as degree-conferring institutions and described themselves simply as schools, continuing under a more modest name to do work which is most useful, but not really academical.

According to official returns, which may be taken as understating rather than overstating the case, seeing that the furnishing of information of the kind cannot be enforced by law, the number of degrees conferred in the United States during the year 1888-89 was as follows:—In classical and scientific colleges, 8,640; in colleges for women, 780; in professional schools, 4,208; honorary degrees, 730. The colleges themselves have been classified in this way:—(1) Those which proceed from the original historical colleges, (2) those established in the name of the State, (3) those avowedly denominational, (4) those founded by private benefactions.

Not more than twelve, and possibly only eight or nine, of the total number of American Universities would, it is thought, be able to stand the application of a rigorous definition of the term. Of the rest the great majority are, as already mentioned, schools in all but name. The position held by some of the leading universities may be inferred from the size of their teaching staffs. In the year named above Harvard had 62 professors, instructors, and lecturers in its collegiate department (excluding theology, law, and medicine); Yale had 46; Columbia, 50; Princeton, 39; Michigan, 47; Johns Hopkins, 49.

A few further particulars may be given. A good point in the American universities, as in those of Scotland and Germany, is that they draw their students from all classes of the community. The subjects which may be taken up by the students show a tendency to increase in number; the 'elective system' has been much discussed in America, and appears to be gaining ground. All the better universities require at entrance a certain minimum of knowledge, whether this is tested by themselves or by the schools from which the students come. There is usually no sharp line of demarcation between pass and honours students; and it is urged that, with some inevitable loss, a good deal is gained by assuming (as the Germans do) that all are at the university to do the best they can, and by not exciting the spirit of competition too greatly. No American university is simply an examining board; attendance at prescribed courses of instruction is, in all, essential to a degree.

The best of the American universities, as has been already said, are glad to learn from those of Germany. They recognise the need of higher and more specialized training, and endeavour to enable their most promising students, by means of Fellowships or Scholarships, to obtain it either at home or in Europe. One of the express objects of the establishment of the Johns Hopkins University was to make provision for 'post-graduate studies,' as the Americans were probably the first to call them. At the opening of this university 20 fellowships (each of the value of £100 per annum) were instituted with the object of "affording to young men of talent from any place an opportunity of continuing their studies in the Johns Hopkins University, while looking forward to positions as professors, teachers and investigators, or to other literary and scientific vocations . . . . . . They are not offered to those who are definitely looking forward to the practice of any one of the three learned professions (though such persons are not formally excluded from the competition), but are bestowed almost exclusively on young men desirous of becoming teachers of science and literature, or proposing to devote their lives to special branches of learning which lie outside of the ordinary studies of the lawyer, the physician, and the minister. Appointments are rarely, if ever, made of graduates of more than five years' standing . . . . . . Every holder of a fellowship is expected to perform such duties as may be allotted to him in connexion with his course of study, to act when called upon as an examiner or as moderator in the examination room, to give all his influence for the promotion of scholarship and good order, and in general to co-operate in upholding the efficiency of the university, as circumstances may suggest. He must reside in Baltimore during the academic year. He may give instruction, with the approval of the president, by lectures or otherwise, to persons connected with the university, but he may not engage in teaching elsewhere." It would seem that 187 fellowships of this kind have been held at the Johns Hopkins University, between the years 1876 and 1888. Of the holders 148, or 79 per cent. of the whole number, have been engaged in teaching, mainly in colleges and universities, while others have given themselves to independent scientific pursuits.

Harvard possesses 24 fellowships, 11 of which do not necessarily entail residence at Harvard, but allow of study at some foreign school of learning. 37 persons held Harvard fellowships in Europe between the years 1873 and 1889. Of these, 10 have filled teaching posts at Harvard, 13 at other colleges and universities, and four at academies and schools; four are engaged in scientific work, one is a preacher, one an orientalist, one a writer, one dead, and two have not yet settled down. "It is a fair question for discussion," says President Eliot, "whether fellowships available in Europe or fellowships available only at the university are most useful. For the purpose of building up a graduate department in a given institution, fellowships available only at that institution are best, but for serving the common cause of education in the country at large there is much to be said for fellowships available in Europe. This university is glad to possess both kinds." It should be added that some of the fellowships at Harvard, Princeton, Cornell, and some other universities, are open to the graduates of other universities. This is the case with all the fellowships of Johns Hopkins, and of the newly-constituted Clark University in Massachusetts.

The fellowship system is comparatively new in America, but it is being rapidly extended, owing to the general appreciation of the success which has attended it. The otal number of fellowships already in existence at various universities and colleges is 147, and the total income attached to them is £13,000 per annum.

It is not only in the encouragement of post-graduate work that the better universities of America show their willingness to learn from those of Germany. Many of the leading American scholars and scientific men have been trained in Germany, and keep up their connexion with it, and with Europe generally, by frequent visits during the summer vacation. Some of us, no doubt, have come across the energetic American professor who hunts up manuscripts in the British Museum or the Continental Libraries, just as at Heidelberg or Leipzig we have also met the wide-awake young American graduate from (say) the University of Wisconsin, who is pursuing his studies at one of those venerable seats of learning. Such men bring home German ideas with them, and we have it on American authority that in recent years German influence has made itself more and more felt in university studies. The Americans do not seem to feel the suspicion of, or contempt for, the German scholar which is often entertained in England. The reason may well be that they have seen more of him, in their own land as well as in his. Many Germans have taught in America, and though they have not always been successful in their dealings with American youths, yet one at least of them (Francis Lieber) did such eminent service to his adopted country that the shortcomings of the rest may readily be forgotten.

Stress has throughout been laid on the conception—the fundamental conception—of a university as a school of learning, because it is one which is apt to fall hopelessly into the background where, as in Wales, London is the best-known type of university. Towards the foundation of such a school of learning, one practical aid will be the institution of university fellowships. Into the conditions under which such fellowships should be held it will not be necessary to enter further than to say that work must be required in all cases, and that in some cases residence abroad should be allowed, so that a student may avail himself of such advantages as those offered at the German universities, or at the Marine Station at Naples, or at the British School of Archæology at Athens.

With this slight exception, the present pamphlet does not aim at being *constructive; suggestive*, however, it is to be hoped it will be on many points, owing to the variety of the information furnished. Summaries, it will be seen, have been prepared of the constitution and general regulations of every British University, including one which has passed out of existence, and another which is not yet in existence and is hardly likely to come into existence in the form in which it is presented here. It may possibly be thought that these might have been omitted; but they have been given partly for completeness, partly because in some respects they show us what to avoid, and partly, too, because where they coincide with accepted models they add at least something to the general agreement. Two at least of those given are unique, unapproachable: Oxford 'spreading her gardens to the moonlight, and whispering from her towers the last enchantments of the Middle Age,' as one of the latest of her great sons has written of her; and Cambridge, as depicted by that still more illustrious poet who, on revisiting the scenes which he and his friend had known together,

> '. . . heard once more in college fanes
> The storm their high-built organs make,
> And thunder-music, rolling, shake
> The prophets blazon'd on the panes.'

Of the Scottish universities, St. Andrews, Glasgow, and Aberdeen are the oldest; while Edinburgh, university and town, is (with its great memories) indeed a 'Modern Athens,' as Louvain was a 'Belgian Athens.' The University of Dublin was, like Edinburgh, founded in Elizabethan times; and it is pleasant to think that an institution which is this year to celebrate its tercentenary has probably never done more brilliant work than during the last few decades.

The Scottish universities perpetuate, in their constitution, the mediæval university organisation; better than that, they have consistently refused to degrade themselves to the level of merely examining bodies; and best of all, they have always shown themselves truly popular universities, and at the same time able to enlist and retain the services of men known throughout Europe for what they have done to extend the frontiers of human knowledge. These and other considerations would seem to mark them out as the natural models for Wales to follow when the time comes for her to organise a university of her own. The difficulty lies in the confederation of the three colleges. The difficulties and dangers inherent in any system of federated colleges in distant towns must be frankly and fully faced, and it must be borne in mind that the practice has not yet stood the test of time. By careful inquiry an effort should be made to ascertain the inner working of any universities organised on this plan—there are but few known examples altogether—with regard to (1) high and uniform standard for degrees, combined with maintenance of the principle that teaching and examining must go together; (2), the existence of real university life and work. Unless these two conditions are fulfilled—unless there is every prospect of securing a high degree standard and advanced work—Wales would do well to wait for her university. It would be grievous indeed if the Welsh University lowered rather than raised our conceptions of higher education. With respect to advanced work, and the standing of the university generally, it will clearly be necessary, if we may once more drive home that point, from the very beginning to apply a fixed proportion of the funds in the way of University Fellowships and Scholarships. Such research and original work, if accomplished, would be one of the best means of raising the degrees of the Welsh University in the general estimation.

It will be the duty of every Welshman who takes an interest in the future of his country to scan closely the draft charter, when it appears, and to ask himself: What does this new machinery give us? Simply degrees, titles, labels? Or does it—we will not say 'give,' for that no machinery can do; does it permit, under favourable conditions, of the growth of a School of Learning in our midst? Does the proposed university add anything to the appliances of learning and the incentives to learning? Does it raise our ideals of learning? Does it mark a definite step forward now, and promise further progress in the future; cr does it mean no advance, but the risk of retrogression?

These questions should be asked by all, but especially by those who indulge the hope that the stream of national feeling which runs high in Wales to-day may prove not simply a force with which the politician has to reckon, and which the manager of men must turn to account, but one which can compel the respect of the best minds of the day. The fulfilment of that hope depends largely on whether all do their best at this time to direct the flood into the right channels, and keep constantly in mind the exhortation printed on the title-page: *Coder safon dysgeidiaeth yn uwch yng ngolwg y wlad.*

NOTES.

A. Table of Dates.

The dates of foundation of the Universities referred to in this pamphlet (with some additions) are as follows :—

12th—15th Centuries.		16th—18th Centuries.		19th Century.	
Bologna	12th century.	Wittenberg (transferred to Halle, 1817)	1502	Berlin	1809
Paris				Bonn	1818
Oxford		Marburg	1527	McGill (Canada)	1821
Cambridge		Königsberg	1544	London	1826
		Jena	1558		
Padua	1222			Munich	1826
		Leyden	1575		
Naples	1225			Toronto (Canada)	1827
		Altdorf (suppressed 1801)	1578		
Salamanca	1243			Durham	1832
		Edinburgh	1582		
Prague	1348			Athens (the modern University)	1837
		Würzburg	1582		
Pavia	1361			Michigan (U.S.A.)	1837
		*Dublin	1591		
Vienna	1365			Queen's University. (Ireland)	1850
		Giessen	1607		
Heidelberg	1386			Sydney (N.S.W.)	1851
		†Strassburg	1621		
Cologne (suppressed 1798)	1388			Melbourne	1853
		Dorpat	1632		
Erfurt (suppressed 1816)	1392			Cornell (U.S.A.)	1865
		Utrecht	1634		
Leipzig	1409			Johns Hopkins (U.S.A)	1867
		Harvard (U.S.A.)	1638		
St. Andrews	1411			New Zealand	1870
		Kiel	1665		
Rostock	1419			Geneva (the modern University, as distinguished from the earlier and famous Academy)	1876
		Halle	1693		
Louvain	1426				
		Yale (U.S.A.)	1701		
Glasgow	1453				
		Breslau	1702		
Freiburg	1455			Amsterdam	1877
		Göttingen	1736		
Greifswald	1456			Royal University of Ireland.	1880
		Erlangen	1743		
Basel	1459			Victoria	1880
		Princeton (U.S.A.)	1746		
Tübingen	1477				
		Münster	1780		
Upsala	1477				
Copenhagen	1479				
Aberdeen	1494				

* Charter granted in 1591, but Trinity College not built and occupied till the following year. Hence celebration of tercentenary in 1892, rather than 1891.

† Originally a Lutheran Academy. From 1681 to 1870 the city was French. German University revived in 1872.

B. **Books.** It has not been found possible, owing to shortness of time and want of access to all the books required, to make the statistics and other information contained in this pamphlet as complete as could have been desired; but in writing the Introduction reference has been made to the following writers and sources :—

(α) GENERAL. S. S. Laurie, *Lectures on the Rise and Early Constitution of Universities.* J. B. Mullinger, *Universities* : Article in Encyclopædia Britannica. Mark Pattison, *Suggestions on Academical Organisation.* Sir William Hamilton's *Discussions* (including reprinted articles on the Patronage and Superintendence of Universities, on the Right of Dissenters to Admission into the English Universities, etc.) J. R. Green, *History of the English People* (Chapter on 'The Universities'). Hallam, *Middle Ages*, vol. iii. Newman, *Idea of a University.* John Stuart Mill, *Inaugural Address at St. Andrews.* Karl Pearson, *The New University for London.* (These trenchant articles, reprinted mostly from the *Academy*, contain much that bears directly upon the conditions of the Welsh as well as of the London problem). Some interesting matter will also be found in the Minutes of Evidence taken before the University for London Commission in 1888. With more special reference to Wales, there is the Report (together with Minutes of Evidence) of the Departmental Committee presided over by Lord Aberdare, the *Traethodau Llenyddol* of Dr. Lewis Edwards (especially 'Yr Hen Brifysgolion a'r Brifysgol i Gymru,' and 'Ysgolion Ieithyddol i'r Cymry'), and the article by Principal T. F. Roberts in 'Y Cymmrodor,' 1890-1, on 'The Proposed University for Wales.'

A popular account of 'Alexandria and her Schools,' and a sketch of 'University Life in Ancient Athens,' will be found in Lectures by Kingsley and Capes, published under those titles. *Minerva: Jahrbuch der Universitäten der Welt* will supply a list of existing universities, together with the names of their teachers, and the number of their students.

(β) GERMAN UNIVERSITIES. It will be seen that the sketch of the German university system follows closely the well-known description in Matthew Arnold's *Higher Schools and Universities in Germany;* but an attempt has been made to bring this up to date by the aid of Conrad's *German Universities for the last Fifty Years* (with *Preface* by Bryce) and other books. A fine estimate of the many-sided importance to Germany of its universities is said to be contained in an Address (which I have not been able to procure) of Dr. Döllinger's, delivered many years ago, and translated into English at the time by Mr. Appleton. The *Bibliographisches Jahrbuch der deutschen Hochschulen* gives a general notion of the literary productivity of the university teachers of Germany.

(γ) AMERICAN UNIVERSITIES. Bryce, *American Commonwealth*, chapter ci.—For the following Reports I am indebted to the kindness of the United States Commissioner of Education: Report of the Commissioner of Education for the year 1888-89 (2 vols.); Reports on the History of Higher Education in the following States:—Massachusetts, Michigan, South Carolina, Georgia, Indiana, Alabama, Wisconsin, Florida; History of Federal and State Aid to Higher Education; Sketch of the History of the College of William and Mary. These are only some of the Reports brought out in a long series with lavish liberality by the United States Bureau of Education.

C. University of Michigan. The following sketch of the early struggles and subsequent development of a new university in a new country may be of interest to many readers in the Principality who are in the habit of looking to the New World for guidance and suggestion. Michigan is selected as being distinctly a favourable example of its kind. It is neither one of the old historical foundations (such as Harvard or Yale), nor a privately-founded or denominational institution, but one which the Acting Commissioner of Education (in forwarding the "History of Education in Michigan," from which the following particulars are taken) describes as "the largest and most successful State university in this country."

The University of Michigan was established at Ann Arbor in the year 1837 by an act of the State Legislature. Its constitution is described as follows:—The government of the university was vested in a board of regents to consist of twelve members and a chancellor who was *ex-officio* president of the board; the members were to be appointed by the governor, by and with the advice and consent of the Senate (*i.e.*, the State Senate). The governor, lieutenant-governor, judges of the supreme court, and chancellor of the State, were *ex-officio* members of the board. The regents had power to enact laws for the government of the university; to appoint professors and tutors; to fix salaries and to appoint a steward and fix the amount of his salary.

The great danger which the university had to overcome at its start lay in an attempt which was made to dissipate its funds among a large number of colleges throughout the State. The advantages of concentration were, however, strongly urged by the leading educators of the country, and their wise counsels fortunately prevailed. In a similar spirit, the board of regents, who had had little or no experience in educational matters, were anxious to spend the bulk of their capital in putting up magnificent buildings; but they were opposed by the Superintendent of Public Instruction, who insisted that able teachers, scientific collections, museums, and libraries were the essentials of a great university, rather than a palatial structure. The Superintendent carried his point, and a good deal was in consequence done to equip the university before it actually started. An entrance examination with a good standard was also established.

For some years, scarcity of funds checked the growth of the young university, but in 1844 things brightened in this respect.

There were, however, other troubles. The students were rebellious ; they formed secret societies ; and when the Faculty attempted to suppress these, its action was thought by public opinion to amount to "an abridgment of the rights of man." The Legislature was apt also to interfere directly in the management of the university. The evils, and their remedy, had been pointed out in the report of a committee appointed in 1840 to inquire into the condition of the university. This report is so justly held to form a landmark in the history of the University of Michigan that we cannot do better than quote the actual words of a portion of it. "When legislatures have legislated directly for colleges, their measures have been as fluctuating as the changing materials of which they are composed. When they have acted under a board of trustees, under the show of giving representation to *all*, they have appointed men of such discordant and dissimilar views that they never could act in concert, so that, supposed to act for and represent everybody, they, in fact, have not and could not act for anybody. What the Legislature should attempt in reference to the University is, in the opinion of the committee, to put the whole subject into the hands of competent men, leaving it with undivided responsibility on their shoulders, and then the Legislature not to meddle with it again except to protect it as guardians, not to destroy it as capricious despots. Repeated legislative interference, known by experience to be the ruin of a cause like this, would soon dishearten every regent who takes an interest or active part in the duties of his office, and the whole plan would soon come to the ground. The duties of the regents, in their turn, will be mostly to provide the means and apparatus and the like, and to fill the various faculties with able men, and throw the undivided responsibility of carrying on the work of education on them. A board of experienced regents can manage the funds of the university better than any legislature, and the faculty can manage the business of education—the interior of the college—better than any regents."

The legislature eventually acted upon these recommendations. Regents were elected directly by the people and invested with full authority during their term of office, and by them the faculty was left a perfectly free hand in its own domain. In this year (1852) the university began, says its historian, a new era in its existence. The management had been transferred to men who were to be elected because of their capacity for dealing with educational matters. They, on their part, were to appoint a President of the University, who was to preside over and guide their own deliberations, but without possessing the right of voting.

The first President, Dr. Tappan, was acquainted with, and an admirer of, the Prussian educational system. His leading aims were: (1) To develop a genuine university of the German type ; (2) As one means to this end, to fill the chairs with specialists, and in appointing the occupants to take no account of denominational considerations ; (3) To maintain identity of standard in the requirements for admission to the various departments of the university; (4) To endeavour to raise the standard of university and school teaching concurrently; (5) To adopt suggested changes gradually, lest sudden transformations should bring destruction rather than improvement.

The university made marked progress under Dr. Tappan's administration; but, unfortunately, in 1857, a new board of regents was elected, consisting of members who had no direct knowledge of the proceedings of the former board, who were otherwise without academical experience, and who fell out with the President and deprived him of his office. Dr. Tappan's memory was fully vindicated at a later time (1874-6), when the board of regents then existing passed resolutions acknowledging his great services in organising the university upon a secure basis, and rescinding and withdrawing any censure, expressed or implied, contained in the resolution which severed his connection with the university. In 1863, a fresh system for electing regents was introduced—one that secured the advantages of retirement in rotation. Eight were appointed; two for two years, two for four years, two for six years, and two for eight. Since that time, elections have been held every two years, for choosing two regents to hold office for eight years.

The university has developed vigorously of recent years, and the State has come to take increasing pride in it, and to give it additional financial support. This success is largely due to the activity of its present President, and to the influence which he commands with the regents and the legislature.

D. Supplementary Notes and Extracts. (a) GERMANY. It will be convenient to give here one or two further notes as to the German educational system. (1) *Abiturientenexamen.* The examination includes (in the case of the Gymnasia) German, Latin, Greek, French; mathematics and physics, geography, history and divinity, Candidates must have been two years in the highest class before presenting themselves for examination. Since 1870 the universities have also been open to youths who have passed the Leaving Examination of *Realschulen* of the first-class. (2) *Privatdocenten.* Since the year 1875 the Prussian Budget has contained an item of £2,700 "for the support of docents or other young men of learning intending to follow a university life." The amount is small, but previously the State made no grant at all for this particular purpose. At Berlin the proportion of *Privatdocenten* to the whole body of teachers is much larger than that indicated in the Introduction as prevailing in the German universities generally. The figures at Berlin are as follows :—Ordinary professors, 98; assistant professors, 87; *Privatdocenten*, 158. Total number of teaching staff, 343. (3) *Finance.* The total cost of education (elementary, secondary, and university) to the Prussian State (not the German Empire) is some £6,000,000 annually. Of this sum about £400,000 is spent on the universities, or between £30 and £40 per student. (4) *Prussian Educational Re-*

vival at the beginning of the present century. It is sometimes said with regard to this that Wilhelm von Humboldt translated into fact the words spoken by Frederick William III. in 1807: " Der Staat muss durch geistige Kräfte ersetzen was er an physischen verloren hat."

(*b*) FRANCE. The universities and colleges were suppressed throughout France at the time of the Revolution. "The University of France (which succeeded to that of Paris) is at present little more than an abstract term, signifying the whole of the professorial body under state control, and comprising various faculties at different centres—Paris, Montpellier, Nancy, etc., together with twenty-seven academical rectorates. Each of these rectors presides over a local ' conseil d'enseignement,' in conjunction with which he elects the professors of lycées and the communal schoolmasters, whose formal appointment is then made by the minister of public instruction."—J. B. MULLINGER. Similarly Prof. Laurie says (in substance): "The ancient University of France has become a mere administrative body under the direct control of the state; the professors and faculties have no independent power, no uniting bond, no common life; and the idea of an autonomous commonwealth, or republic of letters, has utterly disappeared."

The best comments on the above statements (which remain substantially true, notwithstanding recent steps in the direction of decentralization) will be another brace of quotations, one from Mark Pattison, the other from Matthew Arnold:—

(α) "These real and valuable intellectual influences at work in France cannot hide from us the fact that the highest development of scientific culture is not found in that country. It is weak on the side of its university, and that weakness distinctly affects the national character, the position of the country in the world, and its power as the leader of European civilisation. There is a superficiality about the products of French genius which marks the clever but second-rate mind. Clever writers, incomparable talkers, their assertion never carries with it the weight which is derived from known habits of patient and exhaustive investigation. To edit the thoughts of others is their business; the real progress of knowledge is conducted elsewhere. The presence of single names, such as De Sacy and Villoison, Boissonade or Burnouf, proves nothing. They were isolated in their age and country."—*Suggestions on Academical Organisation*, p. 151.

(β) "*Lehrfreiheit* and *Lernfreiheit*, liberty for the teacher and liberty for the learner; and *Wissenschaft*, science, knowledge systematically pursued and prized in and for itself, are the fundamental ideas of the German system. The French, with their ministerial programmes for superior instruction, and their ministerial authorisations required for anyone who wants to give a course of public lectures—authorisations which are by no means a matter of form—are naturally most struck with the liberty of the German universities, and it is in liberty that they have most need to borrow from them. To us ministerial programmes and ministerial authorisations are unknown; our university system is a routine, indeed, but it is our want of science, not our want of liberty, which makes it a routine. It is in science that we have most need to borrow from the German universities. The French university has no liberty, and the English* universities have no science; the German universities have both."—*Higher Schools and Universities in Germany*, p. 152.

(c) THE PROVINCE OF EXAMINATIONS. "The university must have tests of proficiency, to be applied before her degrees and honours are granted. There must therefore be university examinations. On the other hand, it must always be recollected that examinations are a means, not an end; that a good education, a sound and liberal cultivation of the faculties, is the object at which we ought to aim; and that examinations cease to be a benefit when they interfere with this object."—MARK PATTISON, *Suggestions*, p. 246. " I do not say that in countries like Austria and England, where there is so little real love for the things of the mind, examinations may not be a protection from something worse. All I say is that a love for the things of the mind is what we want, and that examinations will never give it."—MATTHEW ARNOLD, *Higher Schools*, p. 149.

(d) THE PRACTICAL END OF A UNIVERSITY TRAINING. "If, then, a practical end must be assigned to a university course, I say it is that of training good members of society. Its art is the art of social life, and its end is fitness for the world. It neither confines its views to particular professions on the one hand, nor creates heroes or inspires genius on the other. Works, indeed, of genius fall under no art; heroic minds come under no rule; a university is not a birthplace of poets or of immortal authors, of founders of schools, leaders of colonies, or conquerors of nations. It does not promise a generation of Aristotles or Newtons, of Napoleons or Washingtons, of Raphaels or Shakespeares, though such miracles of nature it has before now contained within its precincts. Nor is it content, on the other hand, with forming the critic or the experimentalist, the economist or the engineer, though such, too, it includes within its scope. But a university training is the great ordinary means to a great but ordinary end; it aims at raising the intellectual tone of society, at cultivating the public mind, at purifying the national taste, at supplying true principles to popular enthusiasm and fixed aims to popular aspiration, at giving enlargement and sobriety to the ideas of the age, at facilitating the exercise of political power, and refining the intercourse of private life. It is the education which gives a man a clear conscious view of his own opinions and judgments, a truth in developing them, an eloquence in expressing them, and a force in urging them. It teaches him to see things as they are, to go right to the point, to disentangle a skein of thought, to detect what is sophistical, and to discard what is irrelevant. It prepares him to fill any

* These words were written, it should be remembered, twenty-four years ago.

post with credit, and to master any subject with facility.
It shows him how to accommodate himself to others, how to throw
himself into their state of mind, how to bring before them his own,
how to influence them, how to come to an understanding with
them, how to bear with them. He is at home in any society, he
has common ground with every class ; he knows when to speak
and when to be silent ; he is able to converse, he is able to listen ;
he can ask a question pertinently, and gain a lesson seasonably,
when he has nothing to impart himself ; he is ever ready, yet
never in the way ; he is a pleasant companion, and a comrade
you can depend upon ; he knows when to be serious and when to
trifle, and he has a sure tact which enables him to trifle
with gracefulness and to be serious with effect. He has the
repose of a mind which lives in itself, while it lives in the
world, and which has resources for its happiness at home
when it cannot go abroad. He has a gift which serves him in
public, and supports him in retirement, without which good
fortune is but vulgar, and with which failure and disappointment
have a charm. The art which tends to make a man all this
is in the object which it pursues as useful as the art of wealth
or the art of health, though it is less susceptible of method, and
less tangible, less certain, less complete in its result."—*Newman,.
Idea of a University*, p. 177.

E. **Beth yw Prifysgol?** Perhaps I may be allowed to reprint
here, from the current number of *Cymru*, a few notes with
regard to the essential characteristics of a university, notes
written with special reference to the case of Wales.

Beth yw Prifysgol? Hawdd yw gofyn, ond nid hawdd ateb,
yn enwedig ar fyr eiriau. Ond y mae'r cwestiwn yn un tra phwysig
i Gymru ar hyn o bryd, ac y mae'n ddyledswydd ar bawb sydd
yn cymeryd dyddordeb mewn addysg uwchraddol ffurfio, hyd
eithaf ei allu, syniadau clir ar y pwnc. Gadawer i ni fraslunio,
yn yr ysgrif fechan hon, ryw fath o ateb i'r gofyniad, a chym-
hwyso yr hyn a ddywedir at amgylchiadau Cymru.

Gyda'r mater hwn, fel gyda llawer ereill, y mae'n haws o lawer
dweyd yr hyn *nad* ydyw'r peth dan sylw na'r hyn ydyw. Yn y
lle cyntaf, y mae'n amlwg mai nid ysgol yn unig yw Prifysgol, pa
un bynnag ai ysgol elfennol ai ysgol ramadegol, ysgol ganolraddol
ai ysgol gelfyddydol, pa un bynnag ai meithrin a choethi'r
meddwl ai parotoi yn uniongyrchol at un o alwedigaethau
bywyd y mae'r ysgol honno. Nis gellir gorbrisio gwerth ysgolion
da o bob math yn y dyddiau hyn ; ond fel y mae'r gair Cymraeg
yn dangos ar ei wyneb, y mae *Prifysgol (Hochschule* yr Almaen-
wyr) yn rhywbeth mwy nag ysgol,—yn ysgol yr ysgolion.

Nid Swyddfa Addysg yw Prifysgol ychwaith. Y mae Swyddfa
o'r fath yn ddefnyddiol mewn unrhyw wlad ; ond nid Bwrdd i
gyfundrefnu'r holl addysg a roddir o fabandod i oedran gwr yw
Prifysgol fel y cyfryw. Gwnaiff Prifysgol hen a chref,—Caer
Grawnt, er engraifft,—waith lawer yn y cyfeiraid hwn, am fod
ganddi ei gwala a'i gweddill o athrawon : bydd gan hyd yn nod

Brifysgol ieuanc ddylanwad mawr ar gyfundrefn addysg yn ei
gwahanol ganghennau; ond er hynny, cofier mai nid amcan
pennaf nac angenrheidiol Prifysgol yw arholi'r ysgolion.

Ac yn olaf, nid corff i roddi graddau yw Prifysgol; o'r hyn
lleiaf, nid hanfod Prifysgol yw hyn, ond yn hytrach swydd
ddefnyddiol a gyflawnir ganddi. Mae gradd yn arwyddlun, ond
nid yn ddiben: yn nod, ond nid yn gyrchnod. Ar Brifysgol
Llundain y gorwedd y bai am ddyryswch lawer ynglyn a'r mater
yma ym meddwl y bobl, ond nid Prifysgol yng ngwir ystyr y
gair ydyw Llundain. Ni chyfranna addysg o gwbl, ni wna ond
arholi.

Beth, ynte, yw Prifysgol? Prifysgol ydyw corfforaeth,—dyna
a olygir gan y gair *university, universitas*,— o ddynion hen ac
ieuainc, athrawon a disgyblion, yn cyd-ddysgu ac yn dilyn
gwybodaeth er ei mwyn ei hun i ba le bynnag yr arweinio;
dynion sydd yn dal o flaen y wlad syniadau cywir am y ddysg
uchaf, tra y maent hwy eu hunain yn gwneyd yr hyn a allont i
eangu terfynau gwybodaeth. Llenwir hwy, os ydynt yn deilwng
o'u galwad, ag ysbryd dysg a chariad at ddysg, a thraddodant i
ereill lamp gwybodaeth fydd a'i goleuni'n disgleirio'n fwyfwy o
genhedlaeth i genhedlaeth. Pe ceid y fath ddynion yng
Nghymru, wedi to neu ddau, nis gallent lai na dyrchafu safon
addysg trwy'r wlad. Nid oes yn y byd heddyw brifysgolion mor
enwog ag eiddo'r Almaen; a'u gogoniant arbennig hwy ydyw y
llu o gyd-efrydwyr sydd yn ffurfio un corff ac yn cyd-weithio o
hyd.

Ond a oes gobaith y ceir Prifysgol o'r fath yng Nghymru o
gwbl? Oes, yn ddiau, os bydd i'r ysbryd cenedlaethol, â'r
hwn y cysylltir mor agos fywyd y sefydliad, brofi ei hun yn
oleuedig a chraff. Y mae'r ysbryd hwnnw'n gryf; ac arno, i
raddau pell, y dibynna 'r dyfodol. Y mae hyd yn nod yr efrydydd
distaw yn ei lyfrgell yn teimlo'r llanw'n codi; ac y mae'n
gobeithio y caiff weled llong dysg yn nofio'n falch ar y tonnau.
Ond ar yr un pryd y mae peryglon i'w gwynebu. Yn gyntaf oll,
y mae perygl i ni orlwytho'r Brifysgol newydd nes iddi suddo.
Cymerer arholi ysgolion canolraddol yn engraifft; oni fyddai'n
ddoeth i Bwyllgor Canolog Addysg Ganolraddol ymgymeryd â'r
gwaith ei hunan,—gyda chynhorthwy athrawon y Brifysgol os
mynnir,—yn hytrach na'i drosglwyddo i'r Brifysgol heb ystyriaeth
bwyllog?

Ni fydd yr un Brifysgol Gymreig yn wir genedlaethol na fo'n
agored i bawb heb wahaniaeth barn a sefylifa a rhyw, ac na fo
hefyd yn rhoddi lle anrhydeddus i efrydiaethau Cymreig. Dylai
arweinwyr y bobl fynnu y pethau hyn; ond dylent fod yr un mor
eiddigeddus dros beth arall sy'n llawn mor agos at anrhydedd y
Cymry, sef safon a nodwedd graddau'r Brifysgol. Gwyddis fod
graddau llawer Prifysgol yn yr Amerig wedi myned yn wawd ac yn
ysgydwad pen; a hawdd y gellir dychymygu effeithiau galarus ar
holl gyfundrefn addysg pan ostyngir yr hyn a gyfrifir yn uchaf.
Mae'n wir mai oes dyngarwch yw ein hoes ni; ond ni ddylai'r
teimlad hwnnw ymestyn hyd at raddau y Brifysgol. Er mwyn

cadw'r safon yn uchel, bydd yn anhebgorol angenrheidiol i'r
colegau gydweithio'n galonnog ac unfrydol, a chael eu dal ynghyd
â rhwymyn cryf, a'u cefnogi gan farn y cyhoedd.
 Dylai efrydiaethau y Brifysgol fod yn rhyddfrydig ac eang, fel
un ffordd i'n gwneyd yn fwy hynaws tuag at y rhai nad ydynt
o'r un farn a ni. Ni fyddant yn wir genedlaethol oni
chynhorthwyant ni i orchfygu rhyw ychydig ar ein chwerwder
enwadol a gwleidyddol. Dylent hefyd fod yn ddwfn a thrwyadl.
Dywedir llawer, a chyda gwirionedd perffaith hefyd, am y fantais
o fod yn bobl ddwyieithog. Ond tra yn defnyddio'r manteision
hyn i'r eithaf ni ddylem anghofio nac esgeuluso'r demtasiwn i
fod yn arwynebol sydd mor barod i amgylchu pobloedd a phersonau
a lefarant fwy nag un iaith. Dylid hefyd, yn drydydd, gydnabod
mai er ei mwyn ei hun y ceisir gwybodaeth mewn prifysgol.
Mae gwlad fechan, fel Cymru neu Switzerland, a drig yn agos
at gymydogion cryf, yn dra thebyg o edrych ar addysg i ryw
raddau mewn ysbryd masnachol; ond ni ddylai'r ysbryd hwnnw
gael dyfod i mewn i ddirgelfa y Brifysgol. Wrth gwrs, nid yw 'r
perygl hwn yn gyfyngedig i un wlad; y mae'r oes ei hun yn
fasnachol; hyd yn nod yn yr Almaen gorfodir i'r athrawon
rybuddio 'r myfyrwyr yn gyson rhag *Brodstudien* ("efrydiaethau
bara.") Ond nid gwir natur y Cymry yw hyn; ac o'm rhan i,
disgwyliwn weled Prifysgol deilwng o'r enw yng Nghymru,—os
bydd Cymru yn ffyddlawn iddi ei hun,—yn gynt nag yn Llundain,
lle sonnir cymaint yn y dyddiau hyn am "Brifysgol i Ddysgu."
 Y mae hyn oll yn ein harwain at y pwnc olaf, sef sefydlu
Cartref Dysg yng Nghymru. Dyma hanfod Prifysgol; a dyma'r
diben y rhaid ei gadw mewn golwg o'r dechreu wrth drefnu ochr
ariannol y Brifysgol. Gwelwyd hyn yn eglur gan Dr. Lewis
Edwards flynyddoedd yn ol. Yn ei draethawd ar "Yr hen
Brifysgolion a'r Brifysgol i Gymru," rhoddodd ei farn i'r perwyl
hwn,—" Bydd yn rhaid cael rhyw fanteision neillduol nas gellir
eu cyrraedd ond mewn cysylltiad â'r sefydliad hwn [h.y., y
Brifysgol Gymreig]. Yr hyn a olygwn ydyw nifer o *fellowships*
i'r rhai fydd yn sefyll uchaf yn niwedd eu hefrydiaeth.
Gwyddom mai ofer fyddai son am hyn wrth y Cymry yn
gyffredin. Ni wnaent ond hwtio y meddylddrych ar unwaith.
Ond y mae blaenoriad yr ysgogiad hwn yn gwybod yn well am
natur prifysgolion. Gwyddant hwy mai dyma un o elfennau
cryfder yr ysgolion pennaf yn y deyrnas, a'u bod yn amcanu at
hyn yn awr yn Edinburgh. Ond beth bynnag am ysgolion
ereill, nid yw ond ffolineb son am brifysgol Gymreig heb *fellowships*. Dylai y *Fellows* gael rhan yn llywodraethiad y Brifysgol,
a gallai rhyw nifer o honynt gael cyflog ychwanegol fel
cynhorthwywyr i'r athrawon sefydlog."
 Yr oedd Dr. Edwards yn llygad ei le, fel arferol; y *mae*'n
ffoliueb son am Brifysgol Gymreig heb *fellowships*. Ni ddylai y
Cymmrodoriaethau neu Ysgoloriaethau Prifysgol, fel y gellid eu galw,
fod yn rhai bras; gellir disgwyl i Gymro aberthu rhyw ychydig
ar allor gwladgarwch a chariad at ddysg. Ni ddylai, ychwaith,
yr un o honynt fod yn segur, ond dylai fod i'r rhai a'u daliant

amodau pendant o waith, pa un ai fel cynhorthwywyr ai fel ymchwilwyr i ryw gangen o wybodaeth gartref, ai fel efrydwyr yn Ffrainc neu'r Almaen, yn Athen neu yn Naples. Os tueddir neb i ameu defnyddioldeb yr ysgoloriaethau hyn, cymhared Goleg y Drindod, Dublin, â Phrifysgolion yr Alban, gyda golwg ar eu hysgol glasurol er engraifft; a thynned ei gasgliadau ei hun. Yn Victoria, dechreuwyd heb ysgoloriaethau o'r fath, ond y mae'r camgymeriad yn awr yn cael ei gywiro: gwell hwyr na hwyrach.

Yn ychwanegol at Ysgoloriaethau, bydd yn angenrheidiol i ni apelio at y Llywodraeth, yn gystal ag at haelioni cyhoeddus, am arian i wellhau ein Llyfrgelloedd, a'n Hamgueddfeydd, a'n *Laboratories*. Yn y Gymraeg,—Iaith, Hanes, a Llenyddiaeth,— mae gobaith am waith da i attynnu sylw y cyfandir hwyrach; yn Saesneg,—Llenyddiaeth a Hanes,—y mae llawer o bethau i'w harchwilio o safle'r Cymro: ac am y gwyddorau, heblaw gwneyd eu gwaith eu hunain, rhoddant, trwy eu dull o weithio a'u hegni, symbyliad i ymdrechion mewn canghennau ereill.

Os nad wyf yn camgymeryd yn fawr, nid ymfoddlona gwladgarwch Cymreig ar ffug Brifysgol, ar y cysgod heb y sylwedd. Ac os ceir y peth iawn, yna bydd cenedlaetholdeb Cymreig wedi ennill iddo ei hun barch y goreuon ym mhobman am iddo wneyd nid ychydig i ddyrchafu pobl gyfan.

W. RHYS ROBERTS.

Coleg Prifysgol Gogledd Cymru.
Mehefin 15, 1892.

ENGLAND.

I. University of Oxford.
SUMMARY OF CONSTITUTION, DEGREE REGULATIONS, ETC.

I. Officers.
1. *The Chancellor*—an honorary official chosen by Convocation and holding office for life.
2. *The Vice-Chancellor.*
    α. *Appointment.*
    Appointed every year by the Chancellor, who, however, adheres to the rule of selecting the Heads of Colleges in rotation of seniority, each Head holding the post for 3 successive years.
    β. *Powers.*
    Acts as Chairman and President of the three legislative bodies—the Hebdomadal Council, Congregation, and Convocation.
3. *Two Proctors.*
    α. *Appointment.*
    Appointed every year by two Colleges in fixed order of rotation : no one can be proctor twice.
    β. *Powers.*
    i. Control the discipline of the Undergraduates (fines, rustication).
    ii. Serve on all Boards and Delegacies.

II. Legislation.
There are *three* legislative bodies :—
1. *The Hebdomadal Council.*

1. The Vice-Chancellor.	1
2. The Proctors	2
3. Six Heads of Colleges	6
4. Six Professors	6
5. Six Masters of Arts	6
	21

N.B.—The Heads, Professors, and Masters are elected, each for six years, by voting in Congregation, half retiring every three years.

2. *Congregation.*
   All Masters of Arts resident at the University.
3. *Convocation.*
   All Masters of Arts, resident or non-resident, who by paying university dues have kept their names 'on the books.'

Convocation is the supreme governing body of the University, whose approval is necessary for all statutes, decrees, and money grants; but in practice the power is mainly in the hands of (i.) the Hebdomadal Council, which *originates* every measure, (ii.) Congregation, which can *amend* bills, while Convocation can only *accept* or *reject*.

[The Hebdomadal Council can, however, be compelled to draw up and submit a proposed decree to Congregation, if a certain number of Masters of Arts sign a requisition to that effect].

a. All University '*statutes and decrees*' must pass through the following stages :
   i. Be initiated by the Hebdomadal Council.
   ii. Pass two readings in Congregation, in the second of which *amendments* may be introduced.
   iii. Be accepted or rejected in their amended form by Convocation.

N.B.—No member of Congregation or Convocation can introduce a bill of any sort before those bodies (this can only be done by the Hebdomadal Council) but any member of Congregation may propose amendments to a bill already introduced.

β. '*Money Grants*' have to pass through stage i. only before being submitted to Convocation.

III. Administration.

While Convocation and Congregation legislate there are a number of elective boards, responsible to Convocation and Congregation, which actually carry out the details of administration. These are

1. For *Teaching* purposes.

The '*Faculty Boards*,' one for each Faculty [Arts, Science, Medicine, History, Theology, Law, Oriental Languages].
- a. *Composition.*
    - i. The Professors in each subject included in the Faculty.
    - ii. Representatives chosen by the body of recognised Teachers in each subject included in the Faculty.
- β. *Powers.*
    - i. Fixing the details of degree curricula, so far as this can be done without infringing the Statutes dealing with the Faculty in question. [*e.g.*, the History Board can settle the length of periods, or the number of special subjects, but could not require candidates offering Modern History to have taken Honour Moderations, or not to have exceeded 14 terms since Matriculation].
    - ii. Electing three or four delegates, who, with the Vice-Chancellor and Proctors, form the Board of Nomination which appoints examiners for the Faculty in question.

2. For *Financial* purposes the 'Delegacy of the Common Fund,' which disposes of the contributions of the Colleges to joint university purposes.

3. For *other* purposes a number of Delegacies, such as 'Curators of the Parks,' 'Curators of the School Buildings,' 'Delegates of Lodging House Inspection,' 'of University Extension,' 'of Public School Examinations,' etc.

IV. Degrees.

1. *Honorary*, granted by *Convocation*.

2. *Ordinary*, granted by the "*The Antient House of Congregation*," which represents the old teaching staff of the University and must not be confounded with *Congregation*. This House consists of:—
   1. Professors.
   2. Resident Doctors in all Faculties.
   3. Resident Masters of Arts under ten years' standing.
   4. Examiners.
   5. Heads and Deans of Colleges and Halls.

Degree Course.

1. Matriculation.

A student becomes an undergraduate member of the University by being admitted into some College or Hall, or into the Body of Non-Collegiate Students: each of which Societies has its own Entrance Examination. He gains his degree by residing at the University, attending the lectures, and obeying the rules prescribed by the Body into which he has been thus admitted, and passing certain University examinations :—
1. Responsions (vulgarly known as "Smalls").
2. First Public Examination (,, "Moderations").
3. Second Public Examination (,, "Greats").

2. Examinations.

I. Responsions.
1. One Greek Book.
2. One Latin Book.
3. Easy Latin Prose Composition.
4. Arithmetic and *either* Algebra, to Simple Equations, *or* Euclid I.—II.

N.B.—There is now a *Leaving Examination* at most Public Schools, which is accepted in lieu of Responsions.

II. First Public Examination (Moderations).

1. *Divinity.*
    α. One of the Synoptic Gospels, and the Gospel according to St. John, in the original Greek.
    β. The subject matter of the Acts of the Apostles, or of some portion of the Old Testament.
    Or, an alternative subject.
2. *Pass.*
    a. *Classics.*
        i. Three prepared books, one Latin and two Greek, or *vice versâ*.
        ii. Latin Prose Composition.
        iii. Unprepared translation (Greek and Latin).
    β. *Either* (i.) Elements of Logic, Deductive and Inductive.
        or (ii.) Elements of Algebra and Geometry.
3. *Honours.*
    A. *Classical.*
        1. *Prepared translation.*
    α. Translation alone: Homer, Vergil, Demosthenes and Cicero's Orations.
    β. Translation with literary history, criticism, etc., etc. Three or four books selected by the candidate from a fixed list.
        2. *Unprepared translation* (Greek and Latin).
        3. *Composition.*
            α. *Compulsory.* Latin Prose.
            β. *Optional.*
                i. Greek Prose.
                ii. Latin Verse.
                iii. Greek Verse.
4. *Special Subject:* one of the following:—
    1. History of the Greek Drama.
    2. History of Attic Oratory.
    3. History of Roman Poetry.
    4. Elements of Logic, Inductive and Deductive.
    5. Elements of Comparative Philology.

N.B.—Candidates may take an additional subject

instead of Greek Prose, and an additional subject or a fourth book instead of Verse Composition.

    B. *Mathematical.*
1. Algebra and Theory of Equations.
2. Trigonometry, Plane and Spherical.
3. Plane Geometry, including Conics.
4. Differential Calculus.
5. Integral Calculus and Calculus of Variations.
6. Elements of the Mechanics of Solids and Fluids.

N.B. *i.* The Pass and Honours courses are alternative: but a student who takes Mathematical Honours must also pass either in Classical Moderations, or in an additional subject in Responsions.

ii. Candidates must have entered upon their 4th term, and for Honours must not have exceeded their 8th term.

Preliminary Examinations.

Candidates for Honours in any Final School, *may*, instead of Moderations, pass the Law Preliminary or the Science Preliminary, together with an additional subject, and candidates for Honours in Natural Science *must* pass the Science Preliminary, unless they have taken Honours in the First or Second Public Examination.

1. *Law Preliminary.*
    a. Outlines of English History, Political and Constitutional.
    β. Institutes of Justinian, omitting Bk. III., titles 1—12, and IV., 6—18.
    γ. Unprepared Latin Prose translation.
    δ. Either (1) Logic or Bacon's Novum Organum, Bk. I.
    or (2) Greek, French, or German.
        $\begin{cases} a. \text{ Prepared book.} \\ \beta. \text{ Unprepared translation.} \end{cases}$

2. *Science Preliminary.*

The subjects of the Preliminary Examination vary according to the subject chosen for the Final.

The Preliminary subjects are :—
1. Mechanics and Physics.
2. Chemistry.
3. Animal Physiology.
4. Animal Morphology.
5. Botany.

These are required as follows :—

Final Subjects.	Preliminary Subjects.			
1. Physics.	1	2.		
2. Chemistry.	1	2.		
3. Geology or Animal Physiology.	1	2	4	5.
4. Animal Morphology.	1	2	3	5.
5. Botany.	1	2	3	4.

Candidates are admitted at any time after passing Responsions, and may take any number of subjects at the same time.

III. Second Public Examination (Greats).

I. *Pass.*

Three subjects out of the following groups :—

A. *Classical.*
  1. Two books ⎰(α) Portion of a Greek Philosopher.
             ⎱(β)   „   „ Greek or Latin Historian.
  2. Greek and Roman History.
  3. Sanskrit.
  4. Persian.

B. *Modern.*
  1. Period of Modern History and Literature.
  2. French *or* German.
  3. Political Economy.
  4. Branch of Legal study.

C. *Scientific.*
  1. Geometry.
  2. Mechanics.
  3. Chemistry.
  4. Physics.

D. *Religious.*
  1. Passages from Kings and Jeremiah and the First Epistle to the Corinthians.

2. (α) The Nicene Creed, with the Articles XIX.—XXVIII.; *or*
(β) Ecclesiastical History, A.D. 373-407.

3. (α) {Exodus i.—xi. (in Hebrew).
or Exodus i.—xxiv. (in Septuagint).
or Exodus i.—xxiv. and Numbers xi.—xxiv. (in Vulgate).}
or (β) Butler's *Analogy of Religion*, Part I., omitting chapters i. and vi.

Rules for selection of subjects :—
1. Not more than two subjects may be chosen out of the same group.
2. One subject must be a foreign language, *i.e.*, either A (1), A (3), A (4), or B (2).
3. Books or authors may not be selected in which the candidate has passed, either in Responsions or in Moderations.

II. *Honours.*

A. *Literæ Humaniores (Classics).*
1. *Language.* (Greek and Latin).
   α. Prepared books: certain treatises of Plato and Aristotle and of the Greek and Latin Historians.
   β. Unprepared Translation.
   γ. Prose Composition.
2. *History.*
   A period of Greek and a period of Roman History, with the texts selected in § 1.
3. Philosophy.
   α. Political.
   β. Moral   } With the texts selected in § 1, and Bacon's Novum Organum.
   γ. Logic.

"The dominant note of this Examination is in fact general culture upon a firm classical basis."

B. *Mathematics.*
1. *Pure.*
   Algebra, Trigonometry, Geometry of 2 and 3 dimensions, Differential and Integral Calculus, Calculus of Variations and of Finite Differences, Theory of Chances.

2. *Applied.*
   Mechanics of Solids and Fluids, Optics Geometrical and Physical, Astronomy, including elements of Lunar and Planetary Theories.

C. *Modern History.*
   1. *English.*
      α. Constitutional up to 1837.
      β. Political up to 1837.
      γ. One of the following periods to be studied in detail.
         1. 449-1087.
         2. 802-1272.
         3. 1215-1485.
         4. 1399-1603.
         5. 1603-1714.
         6. 1714-1815.
         7. 1760-1848.
   2. *General.*
      One of the following periods corresponding to that selected in English History, and to be studied in connexion with it.
         1. 476-1085.
         2. 936-1272.
         3. 1272-1519.
         4. 1414-1610.
         5. 1610-1715.
         6. 1715-1815.
         7. 1763-1852.

N.B.—The special period must be studied with reference to Social and Literary as well as Political History.

   3. *Special Subject.*
      (1) One of the following:—
         α. Hildebrand.
         β. First Three Crusades.
         γ. Italy, 1492-1513.
         δ. The Great Rebellion.
         ε. India, 1773-1805.
         ζ. The French Revolution to the end of the Convention, 1795.
      or (2) A subject selected by the candidate himself with the approval of the Faculty Board.
      or (3) The History of the Law of Real Property.
   4. *Political Science and Political Economy.* Certain prescribed books.

D. *Law.*
1. Jurisprudence.
2. Roman Law.
3. English Law (including Contracts, Testamentary and Intestate succession, Real Property, and Constitutional Law).
4. History of English Legal and Political Institutions.
5. International Law.

E. *Theology.*
1. *Holy Scriptures.*
   α. General knowledge.
   β. Special books.
   Hebrew may be offered.
2. *Dogmatic and Symbolic Theology.*
   1. The Trinity.
   or 2. The Incarnation.
   or 3. Grace.
3. *Ecclesiastical History and the Fathers.*
   One of the following subjects:—
   (a) The Ante-Nicene Church.
   (b) The Church of the first four Councils (313—451).
   (c) The British Churches to 800.
   (d) The Carolingian Reformation.
   (e) The Papacy in the 11th century.
   (f) The Reformation (1500—16).
   (g) History of Western Canon Law, to the time of Gratian.
4. Evidences of Religion.
   One of the following:—
   Natural Theology and Revelation.
   New Testament Canon.
   Miracles.
   Prophecy.
   Comparison of Christianity with other Religions.

5. *Liturgies.*
6. *Sacred Criticism and Archæology.*

N.B.—For a first-class, the first subject, and three of the remaining five, must be offered. For a lower class the first and any other are sufficient.

F. *Oriental Studies.*
1. Indian Studies.
   a. Languages.
   Sanskrit, Persian, Arabic, Hindustani, Hindī, Marathī, Bengalī, Tamil, Telugu, Chinese, Burmese.
   β. A period of Indian History.
   γ. Special subjects.
   1. Age of Aurangzib (1655-1707).
   2. History of British India (1744-1805).
   3. Administrations of Cornwallis, Shore, and Wellesley (1786-1806).
   4. History and Constitution of the Legislative, Judicial, and Executive Authorities in India.
   5. The Indian systems of Land Tenure and Land Revenue.
   6. Comparison of Buddhism with Brahmanism.
   7. Comparative Grammar of the Aryan Languages of India.
   8. Vedic Philology.

Every candidate must offer (α) Sanskrit, or Persian, or Arabic; (β) a period of Indian History; (γ) a special subject. Candidates who aim at a first-class must also offer (1) two additional languages, or (2) one additional language and one additional special subject.

2. *Semitic Studies.*
I.   a. Arabic.
     β. History of Khalifate and growth of Arabian rule.
     γ. Special subject.
        1. History of Arabic Grammar and Lexicography.

  or 2. History of Arabic Literature to end of 12th Century.
II. *a.* Hebrew.
  β. Jewish History, general and literary, from the return from the Captivity to the seventh century A.D.
  γ. Special subject. Jewish History from the Seventh Century to A.D. 1300.
III. *a. Aramaic.*
  β. Special subjects.
   i. History and character of the Targums.
  or ii. History and character of Syriac versions of the Bible and outlines of Syriac literary history.

Every candidate must offer (1) one language; (2) I. (β) or II. (β); (3) one of the special subjects grouped with the language. Candidates who aim at a first-class must offer a second language together with one of the special subjects grouped with it.

G. *Natural Science.*

 This is rather a group of five Schools than a single School.

I. *Physics.*
  a. General Physics.
  β. Special Subjects.
   One or more of the following:
    (1) Acoustics, (2) Light, (3) Heat, (4) Electricity and Magnetism.

II. *Chemistry.*
  a. Chemical Physics.
  β. Inorganic Chemistry.
  γ. Organic Chemistry.
  δ. General and Theoretical Chemistry.

III. *Geology.*

IV. *Animal Physiology.*
   α. Chemical Functions.
   β. Mechanical Functions.
   γ. Functions dependent on Excitability.
   δ. Generation.

V. *Animal Morphology.*
   α. Comparative Anatomy and Osteology.
   β. Histology and Embryology.
   γ. History of Animal Morphology.

VI. *Botany.*
   (α) General Morphology.
   (β) Special Morphology, of 70 selected types, and the floral structure of 50 plants.
   (γ) Taxonomy and geographical distribution of plants.
   (δ) Vegetable Physiology.

V. Income and Expenditure.

1. Income (in round numbers).

Fees	£30,000
Estates	10,000
Trust Funds	13,000
College Contributions	7,000
Profits of Clarendon Press	5,000
Miscellaneous	1,900
	£66,900

2. Expenditure (in round numbers).

1. Professors	£10,000
2. Other Officers (Librarians, Curators, Examiners, Minor Teachers, etc., etc.)	22,500
3. Bodleian Library	8,000
4. Museum	4,500
5. Interest and Sinking Fund	5,500
6. Miscellaneous (keeping up plant, buildings, etc.)	14,000
	£64,500

[H. R. REICHEL.]

II. University of Cambridge.

Summary of Constitution and of Degree Regulations, etc.

The University of Cambridge is governed by **Statutes** approved in connexion with the Act of 1877, the avowed principle of which was to "enable the University to reform itself." The present Statutes accordingly represent the ideas of University government which prevailed in Cambridge at that time. The most important were, perhaps, (1) the widening of the *curriculum* by introducing new branches of learning; (2) the providing for the needs of the University at the cost of the Colleges.

Popular conceptions of the University are very generally based upon a state of things which has passed away. The University no longer gives special privileges to the study of Mathematics, nor is it dominated by the Colleges. The privileges of the latter are now little more than nominal.

The growth of this University in numbers in recent years is confidently attributed by those who pressed the reforms of the years 1877-82 to the success of their efforts.

The supreme governing body of the University is the **Senate**, or general body of graduates. Meetings are held fortnightly during term time for voting only: discussions are arranged for in the intervals. Owing to the frequency of these meetings the real control rests usually with the resident graduates; but matters of great importance will from time to time bring up great numbers of non-residents. The resident graduates also elect the Council, which alone has the right (at any rate in practice) to initiate legislation; but the Council is usually willing to give the Senate an opportunity of voting on any proposal which is at all largely supported.

The Cambridge degree is only given after **residence**. Attendance at lectures is not demanded: in some subjects the University staff give the teaching required by students: in others it has fallen into the hands of the Colleges or of private tutors.

The connexion between teaching and examination is maintained by **Boards of Studies**, of which there are twelve. The Boards have power to draw up lists of lectures, and to make representations with regard to the studies of the University generally: and such representations usually lead to reforms in the direction indicated.

It is, perhaps, well to notice that Selwyn College is not a constituent college of the University, and is only recognized by the University as a Hall of Residence. Another such hall is conducted by private adventure (Ayerst Hall): and a third by the University itself (Fitzwilliam Hall).

The provisions for election to Professorships are worthy of special attention.

I. Government.

All acts of the University depend on the approval of the **Senate**. All graduates having the degree of M.A., or any higher degree, and paying annual dues to the University (about 17s.), are members.

The **Chancellor** is elected by the Senate. The **Vice-Chancellor** is elected by the Senate, out of two Heads of Colleges nominated by the Council. The **Proctors** are nominated by the Colleges in rotation.

The **Council** is elected by the Electoral Roll, *i.e.*, the resident members of the Senate, one half every two years. Four members must be Heads of Colleges, four Professors, and eight members of the Senate. The Vice-Chancellor is Chairman *ex officio*. The Council has the initiative in all University Legislation : it has also practically the appointment to the offices of Orator, Registrar, and Librarian. In ordinary administration it usually follows the recommendations of Syndicates and Boards of Studies. Syndicates are nominated by the Council itself.

There are twelve **Special Boards of Studies**, and a **General Board**. The special boards consist of the Professors connected with each subject, and such "Readers, University Lecturers, Examiners, and other persons" as the Senate appoints. They are bodies representing the resident teachers of the subjects. The General Board consists of the Vice-Chancellor, one representative of each Special Board, and eight members elected by the Senate. The nomination of Examiners rests in most cases with these boards.

II. Election of Professors, etc.

Most of the Professors are elected by boards specially constituted in connexion with each chair, and continually in existence in case of a vacancy occurring.

The Board consists in each case of

(1) The Vice-Chancellor.

(2) *Eight* persons elected by the Senate, and nominated

Two by the Council.
Three by the General Board of Studies.
Three by the Special Board of Studies.

In order that outside opinion may be represented, each of the Boards of Studies must nominate at least one person not resident in the University nor officially connected with it.

Readers are appointed by the general Board of Studies, subject to the confirmation of the special Board. If the two do not agree, the appointment is made by the Council.

University Lecturers are appointed in the same way: but owing to the small salary offered (usually £50 per annum) the appointments mostly fall to those who are already College lecturers.

III. EXAMINATIONS.

A. For a **Pass** Degree (B.A.), it is necessary to pass in due order

I. The **Previous** Examination, in two parts, which may be taken separately (i.) Greek and Latin, (ii.) Elementary Mathematics, with Paley's Evidences or Logic.

II. The **General** Examination, also in two parts: (i.) Greek, Latin, Algebra, and Elementary Statics and Trigonometry: Latin prose is optional, (ii.) the Acts of the Apostles in Greek, English History and Essay, Elementary Hydrostatics and Heat. A paper on some play of Shakespeare, or on some part of Milton, is optional.

III. The **Special** Examinations. One subject only is required, out of the following :—

Theology.	Chemistry.	Mechanism and
Logic.	Geology.	Applied Science.
Political Economy	Botany.	Music.
Law.	Zoology.	Modern Languages.
History.	Physiology.	Mathematics.
		Classics.

Many of the examinations are in two parts: and students are now encouraged to devote two years to the study of their special subject.

B. For an **Honours** Degree (B.A.), *two* examinations are necessary:

I. The **Previous** Examination, as above; and, in addition, *one* of the following subjects:—Mechanics, French, German.

II. Part I. of *one* of the following Triposes:—Mathematics, Classics, Moral Sciences, Natural Sciences, Theology, Law; or one of the following:—History, Semitic Languages, Indian Languages, Mediæval and Modern Languages.

This is sufficient for a degree, provided that where a Tripos is in two parts it be not passed till the student's third year. An undivided Tripos cannot be passed before the third year, and always qualifies for a degree.

If Part I. of a Tripos is passed in the student's second year, he can obtain a degree by taking either a Special Examination, as above, or the second part of the same Tripos, or the first part of some other Tripos, or an undivided Tripos, at the end of the third year. If Part I. of a Tripos is passed in the third year (as is usually the case), the examinations just named are open to the student in his fourth year, but do not form part of any degree course. The examination in Part II. of each Tripos is of a highly specialized kind, and is divided into numerous sections, one only of which is necessary.

IV. OTHER CONDITIONS FOR DEGREES.

A residence of nine terms is required for a degree. Students of affiliated Colleges, and Extension Lecture students who have attended a continuous course for three years, are excused one year's residence.

The Arts degree is given for Science, Theology, and other subjects as well as for a literary course. The Theological degrees proper are restricted to graduates who are in Holy Orders.

Women are not admitted to degrees, or to any membership of the University. But they are allowed to attend many University lectures, and the Honours Examinations are open to those who have completed the necessary term of residence at Girton or Newnham Colleges.

V. Finance.

The annual income of the University is about £75,000. Of this amount about £25,000 consists of Trust Funds, held on behalf of Professorships, Library, Museums, etc., and principally in the departments of Divinity, Classics, Mathematics, and History. About £35,000 is raised in fees, of which £13,000 is raised by taxing the undergraduate members, and £14,000 by taxing the graduates: the remainder represents examination and lecture fees. Another sum of £13,000 is at present raised by the taxation of the Colleges. From the last two funds University officers and examiners are paid, and large grants are made to newer subjects of study, such as Physics, Chemistry, and Biology. The Local Examinations are self-supporting, having an annual income and expenditure of about £15,000.

The salaries of University officials and professors, though generally higher than those given in the University Colleges of England and Wales, are much lower than those given in the Scotch Universities, and to many of the College officials and lecturers in Cambridge itself.

The annual income and expenditure of the College is about three times as large as that of the University: but space does not permit of my entering upon the subject of its application, except to mention that very large sums are paid to assist the younger members of the University, by way of scholarships and fellowships.

[E. V. Arnold.]

III. University of Durham.

SUMMARY OF CONSTITUTION AND OF DEGREE REGULATIONS, ETC.

This University was established (under an Act of Parliament, passed in 1832) by the Bishop and the Dean and Chapter of Durham, who also drew up the constitution of the University.

The ordinary government of the University is by the Warden (the Dean of Durham), the Senate (consisting of the Professors and Principals of Halls, and six other members of Convocation), and the Convocation. The Convocation consists of the graduates who hold the M.A., or some equivalent or higher degree: its original members were nominated from Oxford and Cambridge graduates.

To obtain a degree in Arts, a residence of two years is required: for a degree in Science, three years' residence at the College of Physical Science at Newcastle-upon-Tyne: for a degree in Medicine, four years' attendance at a medical school, of which only one is necessarily at the Newcastle School of Medicine. Colleges at Barbados and Sierra Leone are affiliated to the University, and residence at these colleges qualifies for a degree. Degrees in Theology are given to persons in Holy Orders only, and not sooner than 10 years after obtaining the B.A. degree.

There are six University Fellowships, each of the annual value of £120, and tenable for eight years: if a fellow takes Holy Orders, of the value of £150, and for ten years. Fellowships are vacated by marriage or preferment. The Warden may, if he please, call upon a fellow to reside and to take part in the examinations of the University.

[E. V. ARNOLD.]

IV. (*a*) University of London.

SUMMARY OF CONSTITUTION.

The University consists of I. Senate.
II. Convocation.

I. Senate.

The Senate consists of
1. *Chancellor*—appointed for life by the Crown.
2. *Vice-Chancellor*—elected for one year by the Senate.
3. *Thirty-six Fellows*—of whom
    a. *Twenty-seven* are appointed directly by the Crown.
    b. *Nine* are chosen by the Crown from a list of persons nominated by Convocation, such list to contain three times the number that are to be chosen at any time.

When vacancies occur, the Crown appoints and Convocation nominates until the above numbers are made up.

There are Five standing Committees of the Senate, of the first four of which, mentioned below, the Chancellor and Vice-Chancellor are *ex-officio* members.

1. Committee on Examinations in *Arts, Science and Law* ... ... 21 members.
2. Committee on Examinations in *Medicine* 9 members.
3. *Library* Committee ... ... 10 members.
4. Committee on the *Examination and Inspection of Schools* ... ... 11 members.
5. Committee on the *Brown Animal Sanatory Institution*.

II. Convocation.

Convocation consists of all graduates of 2 years' standing, who pay an Annual Fee of 5s., or a Life Composition of £1.

Its Powers are:—
1. Nomination of persons as Fellows (3 times as many as are required at any time), from among whom the Crown appoints; the total number thus appointed not to exceed 9, or $\frac{1}{4}$th of the whole Senate.

2. The discussion of matters relating to the University and the declaration of opinion thereon.
3. The decision as to the conditions proposed by the Senate for the recognition of any new degree as a qualification for membership of Convocation.
4. Acceptation of any new or supplemental Charter, or consent to the surrender of an existing Charter.
5. Decision as to the mode of conducting and registering the proceedings of Convocation.
6. Election of a Chairman for a period of 3 years.
7. Election of Member of Parliament.

Convocation *meets* ordinarily once a year (30 a quorum), and has the power of adjournment. An extraordinary meeting may be held at any time at the discretion of the Chairman, provided a requisition, stating the purpose, be made by 20 members. Extraordinary meetings may not be called oftener than at intervals of 3 calendar months.

NOTES.

(a) **Abstract of the Accounts of the University of London from 1st of April, 1889, to 31st March, 1890:—**

1889-90. Dr.	£ s. d.	£ s. d.
To balance on 1st April, 1889		935 12 0
,, Amount received from Paymaster General		14,810 0 0
,, Amount received from Fees, &c., viz. :		
Matriculation	4,807 0 5	
Arts Degree and D.Lit.	4,855 1 6	
Science Degree and Prel. Sc. M.B.	2,920 1 0	
Medical Degrees...	1,617 10 0	
Law Degrees	492 10 6	
Musical Degrees...	82 10 0	
Teacher's Diploma	25 0 0	
		*14,799 13 5
,, Convocation...		161 10 0
,, Provincial examinations	907 15 0	
,, School examinations	196 13 0	
		1,104 8 0
,, Special Endowments, and other Miscellaneous Sources		524 16 4
		£32,355 19 9

		£	s.	d.
*Or calculated otherwise :—				
Matriculation examination	...	4,807	0	5
Intermediate ,,	...	6,300	2	6
Bachelor ,,	...	2,920	0	6
Master and Doctor ,,	...	747	10	0
Teacher's Diploma ,,	...	25	0	0
		£14,799	13	5

1889-90.   CR.

			£	s.	d.
By Amount paid to Exchequer on account of Fees, &c.			15,102	7	0
,,	Amount paid for salaries, wages, and clerical assistance		3,625	11	3
,,	,,	Examiners and Assistant examiners	7,333	2	1
,,	,,	Special and Contingent examiners	779	8	0
,,	,,	Attendants at Practical Examinations	32	7	6
,,	,,	Exhibitions, Scholarships, Prizes, and Medals	1,715	4	8
,,	,,	Expenses at Scientific and Medical Examinations	502	0	0
,,	,,	Re-equipment of Chemical Laboratory	249	16	11
,,	,,	Advertisements	166	15	2
,,	,,	Postage and Carriage of Papers	224	17	3
,,	,,	Convocation Expenses	36	18	9
,,	,,	Petty Cash Expenditure	34	2	4
,,	,,	Library	102	15	10

,,	,,	Deposits—	£	s.	d.			
		Arnott's Exhibitions and Medals	84	3	6			
		Rogers Bequest	18	19	3			
		Provincial Examiners	907	15	0			
		School Examiners	196	13	0			
						1,207	10	9
,,	,,	Income Tax				263	9	6
,,	Balance					979	12	9
						£32,355	19	9

(b) A brief Chronology of the University of London, derived chiefly from the Note on pp. xix. to xxiv. of the Calendar.

1548. Sir Thomas Gresham endowed 7 Professorships, and gave up his house in Bishopsgate for the residence and the lectures of the Professors.

1661. Cowley, influenced by the *New Atlantis* of Bacon, promulgated a scheme for a great London College.

1825. The poet Campbell appealed to the Government of the day urging the foundation of a great London University.

1827. Capital of £160,000 raised to build University College (at first known as the London University).

1828.	Classes in Arts, Law, and Medicine opened in University College.
1829.	King's College received a Charter as a College.
1836.	Charters granted to 1. University College. 2. University of London, with power to grant degrees in Arts, Law, and Medicine.
1839.	Examinations in the Hebrew and Greek Texts of Scripture and in Scripture History established.
1848.	Graduates formed themselves into a Committee for the protection of their general and academical interests.
1850.	Supplemental Charter adding to the number of affiliated Colleges.
1854.	Degree of M.D. recognised as a license to practice.
1858.	Convocation established. Residence at affiliated Colleges no longer demanded as a condition for graduation. Intermediate Examinations introduced.
1860.	Faculty of Science established.
1867.	Special Examinations for Women instituted. The University obtained representation in Parliament.
1870.	New buildings in Burlington Gardens opened.
1878.	Women admitted to degrees on equal terms with men.
1883.	Examination in Art, Theory, and History of Teaching instituted.
1886.	A scheme submitted to the Senate (and the governing bodies of certain other institutions) containing proposals for the establishment of a Teaching University for London. University and King's Colleges jointly appealed to the Crown for power to grant degrees, and submitted a scheme for the establishment of the Albert University. The Royal Colleges of Physicians and Surgeons appealed for permission to grant degrees in Medicine and Surgery.
1888.	A Royal Commission formed to deal with the questions raised.
1889.	Report of Commission issued, recommending that the existing University be widened out, and that the Senate submit a Scheme.
1891.	Draft Scheme issued by the Senate. Rejection of Draft Scheme by Convocation. University and King's College and the London Medical Schools appealed for a Charter of Incorporation into a new University.
1892.	A Royal Commission again appointed to consider the subject.

[R. W. PHILLIPS.]

IV. *(b)* Proposed Albert University.

SUMMARY OF CONSTITUTION.

A. **Faculties.** Arts, Science, Medicine; with power to add others.

B. **Colleges.** University College and King's College. Others may be admitted from time to time. [The Royal College of Physicians (London), and of Surgeons (England), to be associated.]

Medical Schools. Those of University College and King's College. Every other medical school in London recognised by the registering bodies may claim to be admitted as a medical school in the University.

C. **Authorities.**

I. *Chancellor.* Holds office for life. Appointed at first by the Crown. After 10 years the appointment is made by Convocation. Is the head of the University, and may preside over meetings of Council and of Convocation.

II. *Vice-Chancellor.* Must be a member of Council. Holds office for one year. Appointed in the first instance (for 2 years) by the Crown: then by the Council. Exercises all the functions of the Chancellor (in his absence), except the hearing of appeals.

III. *Council,* comprising

[1.] (*a*) the Chancellor.

[6.] (*b*) *Six* persons appointed, in the first instance, by the Crown. Successors during the first 10 years nominated by the Lord President of Council; afterwards, three by the Lord President and three by Convocation.

[12] (*c*) Representatives of University College and King's College (*three for each*) elected by the Councils of the Colleges. [Three representatives each for the Colleges of Physicians and Surgeons.]

[12.] (*d*) Four representatives elected by each of the assemblies of faculties.

On the creation of new faculties, or admission of new colleges, representatives (not more than 4 and 3 respectively) for each such faculty or college will be appointed. The Council to determine the number of such representatives.

Powers. The Council is the governing body and executive: supervises University business, and can do everything allowed by the Charter to be done in the name of the University. In regulating curricula and examinations, it shall proceed only upon recommendation by the assembly of a faculty, or after any plan of its own has been submitted to the assembly of any faculty concerned, for consideration and report.

Members of Council shall hold office for five years, and may be re-elected.

IV. *Assemblies of Faculties,* comprising, for each faculty

(*a*) Teachers giving regular instruction in subjects belonging to the faculty to classes in Colleges of the University. Subject to the approval of the (University) Council, they are to be appointed by the governing bodies of the Colleges to which they belong.

(*b*) Professors, physicians, etc., of the medical schools, appointed (subject, etc., as above) by the governing body of each school.

(*c*) Such examiners in subjects of the faculty as the Council may appoint. [Not to vote on election of members of Council.]

(*d*) Other persons, teaching, or having taught, in London, subjects included in a faculty, may be nominated by the assembly of that faculty, and approved by the Council.

Powers. Elects members of Council (as aforesaid); elects members of Board of Studies for its faculty (see under v.). May discuss and give its opinion on any University matter whatever; may delegate from time to time to its Board of Studies the power of reporting and making recommendations direct to the Council.

V. *Boards of Studies*, comprising for each faculty

(a) Members of the assembly appointed by it from time to time.

(b) Such examiners in the faculty as are members of the assembly.

The Boards of Studies for different faculties may meet in conference, and may jointly or separately report to the Council direct, on matters connected with the faculties.

VI. *Convocation.* Consisting of the Chancellor, Vice-chancellor, and registered graduates.

Powers. Elects Chancellor. Elects three members of Council. May discuss and declare its opinion upon any University matters.

D. Examinations. To be conducted jointly by external examiners and teachers in a college or medical school of the University.

Papers to be submitted, before being set, to a board of examiners.

[G. B. MATHEWS.]

V. Victoria University.

SUMMARY OF CHARTER GRANTED APRIL 20, 1880.

University Court.

(a) *Constitution of:—*

The Chancellor. Appointed in first instance by the Crown: subsequent appointments made by Convocation: holds office for life.

The Vice-Chancellor. Appointed in first instance by the Crown: subsequent appointments made by University Court: holds office for two years: re-eligible.

Twelve persons appointed by the Charter: their successors appointed by the Lord President of the Council. Six hold office for life, three for six years, and three for three years.

Three persons appointed by the Chancellor.

Four persons elected by Convocation. These (as well as the three persons appointed by the Chancellor, and other members of the Court) to hold office for a period to be determined by Statute, and not to exceed twelve, or be less than three, years.

The President,
The Chairman of the Council, } Of each College in the University.
The Principal,

Not less than two or more than four persons chosen by and from the members of the Senate of each College.

Not less than four or more than twelve persons chosen by the governing body of each College.

> [Exact amount of representation in the two last cases to be fixed by the University Court: but Owens College, with which the University opened, to have the full number of representatives above mentioned. The total number of members of the Court is close on sixty.]

(*b*) *Powers of:*—

The University Court is the governing body of the University. It has full power to make and alter or revoke statutes for regulating all matters concerning the University.

University Council.

(*a*) *Constitution of:*—

The Chancellor.

The Vice-Chancellor.

Six members of the University Court, appointed in this behalf by the Lord President of the Council.

Two other members of the Court chosen in this behalf by the Court from among such of its members as are elected by Convocation.

Four other members of the Court chosen in this behalf by the Court.

The President,
The Chairman of the Council, } Of each College in the University.
The Principal,
The Professors who represent the Senates on the Court.

> [Periods of office of members of Council to be determined by statute.—Actual total of members of the Council: 31].

(*b*) *Powers of* :—

The University Council is the Executive body of the University. But (1) not competent to include or exclude Colleges; (2) decisions subject to appeal, on part of individual member, to Court.

[*Meetings of Court and Council.* There are two fixed meetings of the Court, six of the Council, in each year.]

Convocation.

(*a*) *Constitution of* :—

Chancellor, Vice-Chancellor, Professors, Lecturers, and registered Graduates of the University for the time being.

(*b*) *Powers of* :—

Election of Chancellor and of certain members of University Court, etc. Declaration of opinion on any matter whatsoever relating to the University. Regulation of own proceedings, etc.

General Board of Studies.

The General Board of Studies to consist in the first instance of the Professors of Colleges of the University, together with the External Examiners; afterwards, of the Professors and Examining Lecturers, together with the External Examiners. The General Board to present to the Court a report as to the organization of Special or Departmental Boards of Studies in the University.

Examiners, Degrees, etc.

The Examiners of the University to be the Professors of the University, with such Lecturers of the University as the University Court on the report of the General

Board of Studies from time to time appoints, and External Examiners appointed from time to time by the University Council. All regulations as to External Examiners, Examinations, Degrees, and distinctions, to be made by the University Court after considering a report of the General Board of Studies thereon.

Admission of Colleges.

The University Court, after considering a report to be made in each case by the University Council, may accept the application of any incorporated College to be admitted as a College in the University on the Court being satisfied :—

(1) That the College applying has established a reasonably complete curriculum, and possesses a reasonably sufficient teaching staff in the departments of Arts and Sciences at least.

(2) That the means and appliances of the College for its teaching are established on a sound basis, and

(3) That the College is under the independent control of its own Governing Body.

NOTES.

(*a*) **Leading features.**—"The characteristic features of the Victoria University, as compared with other British Universities, are these: (*a*) it does not, like London, confer its degrees on candidates who have passed certain examinations only, but it also requires attendance on prescribed courses of academic study in a college of the University; (*b*) the constitution of the University contemplates its (ultimately) becoming a federation of colleges ; but these colleges will not be situated, like those of Oxford and Cambridge, in one town, but wherever a college of adequate efficiency and stability shall have arisen. University College, Liverpool, and the Yorkshire College, Leeds, having fulfilled these requirements, have become affiliated with the University. The University, like the older bodies in England and Scotland, is at once a teaching and an examining body, and there is an intimate *rapport* between the teaching and the examining functions. To give it a general or national character, the governing body consists partly of persons nominated by the Crown and partly of representatives of the governing and teaching bodies of the colleges and of the graduates of the University. External examiners are appointed, who conduct the examinations in conjunction with examiners representing the teaching body. The graduates of the University meet its teachers in convocation to discuss the affairs of the University. Convocation will elect future chancellors, and a certain number of representatives on the court."—Thompson, *The Owens College*, p. 548. It should be added that Victoria exhibits a revolt against London, not only in requiring residence, but also in allowing a greater choice of subjects in its degree examinations.

(*b*) **Finance—University Scholarships and Fellowships.**—The accounts of the Victoria University are not published. Provision is made for encouraging original research by means of postgraduate Scholarships and Fellowships.

(*c*) **Departmental Boards of Studies.** These are seven in number, and in each case include the Vice-Chancellor, and the Chairman and the Deputy Chairman of the General Board of Studies, in addition to the members named below.

    I. *Board of Languages.* The Examiners of the University in Classics, History, and Modern Languages.
    II. *Board of History and Philosophy.* The Examiners in History, Philosophy, Political Economy, and Classics. The Professors of Law and Jurisprudence.
    III. *Board of Mathematics and Engineering.* The Examiners in Mathematics, Physics, and Engineering. The Professors of Geology.
    IV. *Board of Experimental Science.* The Examiners in Physics, Chemistry, Physiology, Geology, and Mineralogy. The Professors of Mathematics and Professor Reynolds (Professor of Engineering).
    V. *Board of Biology.* The Examiners in Physiology, Botany Zoology, and Geology. The Professors of Chemistry and Anatomy.
    VI. *Board of Law.* The Examiners in Law and Jurisprudence The Professors of Latin, History, and Philosophy.
    VII. *Board of Medicine and Surgery.* The Examiners in Medicine and Surgery. The Professors of Physics, Chemistry, Zoology, and Botany.

(*d*) **Residence.** Candidates for the Ordinary Degrees of B.A. and B.Sc. are required to furnish certificates of having passed through, in a College of the University, a course of study approved by the University, extending over at least three academic years, corresponding to the Preliminary, the Intermediate, and the Final Examinations respectively, of which years at least two shall be subsequent to the date at which they have passed the Preliminary Examination.

But any candidate who has passed the Preliminary Examination next after his matriculation, and has been placed in the First Division, may take his degree of B.A. or B.Sc. after two years of academical study from the date of such Preliminary Examination.

(*e*) **Graduation.** The Degrees in the Faculties of Arts and Science are Bachelor of Arts and Bachelor of Science, Master of Arts and Master of Science, together with a Degree of Doctor, viz., Doctor of Literature, Doctor of Philosophy, or Doctor of Science.

Degree of Bachelor in Arts or Science.

There are three Examinations for the Degree of Bachelor: the Preliminary, the Intermediate, and the Final.

At the **Preliminary Examination** candidates must satisfy the Examiners in five subjects as follows:—
1. English Language and English History (including Geography).
2. Mathematics.
3, 4, 5. *Three* of the following, *one* of which must be a language:
       i. Greek.
       ii. Latin.
       iii. French.
       iv. German.
       v. Elementary Mechanics.
       vi. Chemistry.
       vii. Physiography.

At the *Intermediate Examination and Final Examinations* candidates must satisfy the Examiners in the following subjects:

Intermediate Examination in Arts.
1. Pure Mathematics *or* Logic.
2. Ancient History *or* Modern History.
3, 4. *Two* of the following languages, *one* of which must be Greek or Latin.
       i. Greek.
       ii. Latin.
       iii. French.
       iv. German.
       v. Italian.
       vi. English.
5. Applied Mathematics, or Physics, or English Literature, or *one* of the subjects named in 1, 2, 3, or 4, not already selected.

Final Examination in Arts.
1. English Literature.
2. Greek or Latin, provided that candidates taking two modern languages in 3, 4, may substitute a third modern language for either Greek or Latin.
3, 4. *Two* of the following:—
       i. *Greek with Greek History *or* *Latin with Roman History.
       ii. French Language and Literature.
       iii. German Language and Literature.
       iv. Italian Language and Literature.
       v. English Language.
       vi. History, Ancient and Modern.
       vii. †Modern History, with Political Economy, *or* Political Economy, with Economic History.
       viii. Pure Mathematics.

*If not taken under 2.
† If not taken under vi.

ix. Applied Mathematics.
x. Philosophy.
xi. *History of Philosophy.

Intermediate Examination in Science.

1, 2, 3. *Three* of the following:—
    i. Pure Mathematics.
    ii. Applied Mathematics.
    iii. Physics.
    iv. Chemistry.
    v. Biology.
    vi. Applied Mechanics *or* Surveying.

Provided that of the three subjects selected, *one* shall be Pure Mathematics or Applied Mathematics or Biology.

Final Examination in Science.

1, 2. *Two* of the following:—
    i. Pure and Applied Mathematics.
    ii. Physics.
    iii. Chemistry.
    iv. Zoology.
    v. Botany.
    vi. Physiology.
    vii. Geology.
    viii. Mental and Moral Science.
or ix., x. Engineering.

3. *One* of the following, to be presented at *either* the Intermediate *or* the Final Examination, the standard being that of the Intermediate Examination in either case:—
    i. †Applied Mathematics.
    ii. Logic.
    iii. French Language.
    iv. German Language.
    v. English Literature.
    vi. ‡Applied Mechanics.
    vii. ‡Surveying.

Degree of Bachelor in Arts or Science with Honours.

The Honours Schools of the University are the following:

Faculty of Arts.
    i. Classics.
    ii. History.
    iii. English Language.
    iv. Philosophy.

* Candidates selecting two classical languages will be examined in the History of *Ancient* Philosophy only.
† If not presented at Intermediate Examination.
‡ If not presented at Intermediate Examination or under ix., x. of 1, 2 above.

Faculty of Science.

      v. Mathematics.
     vi. Engineering.
    vii. Physics.
   viii. Chemistry.
     ix. Zoology.
      x. Physiology.
     xi. Geology, Mineralogy, and Palæontology

The names of those who have passed in Honours are drawn up in three classes, and each class is arranged in alphabetical order.

Those who take the above schools are required to pass the Preliminary Examination (Ordinary) and the Final Honours Examination only. There is no Intermediate Examination.

Degree of Master in Arts or Science.

The degree of Master is conferred upon Bachelors of Arts or Science, who are of three years' standing, as follows :—(1) If they have graduated with Honours, without further examination ; (2) if they have not so graduated, after satisfying the examiners in such portions of the examination in some Honours School of the University, as the General Board of Studies may from time to time approve.

Degree of Doctor in Literature, in Philosophy, or in Science.

The degrees of Doctor of Literature, Doctor of Philosophy, and Doctor of Science are conferred by the University upon registered Masters of Arts or Masters of Science of the University who shall be deemed by the Council, on a report furnished by the General Board of Studies after considering a report from one or more of its Departmental Boards, to have distinguished themselves by special research or learning.

Provided that the General Board of Studies may, in such cases as shall think fit, after considering a report from one or more of its Departmental Boards, also require candidates to *pass such an examination as it may from time to time determine.

In all cases not less than six years must have elapsed since the date of admission to the Bachelor's Degree.

[W. RHYS ROBERTS].

SCOTLAND.

I. University of Edinburgh.

Summary of Constitution, and of Degree Regulations in Arts and Science, etc.

The Governing Bodies are three in number:— The Court; The Senate; The General Council. The Governing Bodies. Their number.

THE COURT consists of The Rector; The Principal; The Lord Provost of Edinburgh; An Assessor nominated by the Chancellor; An Assessor nominated by the Rector; An Assessor nomimated by the Municipality of Edinburgh; Four Assessors elected by the General Council; Four Assessors elected by the Senate; Representatives, not exceeding four in all, of such Colleges as may hereafter be affiliated with the University. Their Constitution.

THE SENATE consists of the Principal and Professors of the University.

THE GENERAL COUNCIL consists of the Chancellor, the members of the University Court, the Professors, the Graduates, and all persons who previous to 2nd August, 1861, had, as matriculated students, given regular attendance on the course of study in the University for four complete sessions, the attendance for at least two of such sessions having been on the course of study in the Faculty of Arts.

THE COURT.—(1) Administers and manages the whole revenue and property of the University. (2) Their Functions. The Court.

Reviews any decision of the Senate on a matter within its competency which may be appealed against by a member of the Senate, or other member of the University having an interest in the decision. (3) Reviews on representation made by any of its members, or by any member of the Senate, any decision which the Senate may come to in the exercise of its powers; but has no power to review any decision of the Senate in a matter of discipline, except upon appeal taken either by a member of the Senate or by a member of the University directly affected by such decision. (4) Appoints professors whose chairs are in the patronage of the University; appoints examiners and lecturers; grants recognition to the teaching of any college or individual teacher for the purposes of graduation under regulations laid down by the Commissioners appointed under the Universities (Scotland) Act, 1889, which regulations after the expiration of the powers of the Commissioners may from time to time be modified or altered by the Universities Committee. (5) Defines, on application by any member of the Senate, the nature and limits of a professor's duties under his commission, subject to appeal to the Universities Committee. (6) Takes proceedings against a principal or professor, university lecturer, assistant, recognised teacher, or examiner, and has power to call before it any member of the University to give evidence, and to institute and conduct any such inquiries as it may deem necessary. (7) Appoints one-third of the members of any standing committee charged with the immediate superintendence of any libraries or museums, belonging to the University and Colleges, and reviews any decision which the Senate may come to in respect of the recommendations of such committees. (8) Has power after the expiration of the powers of the present commissioners to found new professorships with the approval of the Universities Committee.

THE SENATE (1) superintends and regulates the teaching and discipline of the University. (2) Appoints two-thirds of the members of any standing committee charged with the immediate superintendence of any libraries or museums belonging to the University, receives, in the first instance, the reports of such committees, and subject to the review of the University Court, confirms, modifies, or rejects the recommendations in such reports. (3) Recommends candidates for degrees in Arts, Divinity, Law, Medicine, and Science. (*Note.* The degrees are conferred by the Chancellor, Vice-Chancellor, or Principal, on the recommendation of the Senate.) The Senate.

THE GENERAL COUNCIL (1) elects the Chancellor and four of the Assessors in the University Court, (2) holds meetings for the consideration of all questions affecting the well-being and prosperity of the University, and makes representations from time to time on such questions to the University Court. (An ordinance of 1858 requires that all proposed improvements in the internal arrangements of the University " shall be submitted to the University Council for consideration.") (3) Returns a Member of Parliament jointly with the General Council of theUniversity of St. Andrews. The General Council.

CURATORS OF PATRONAGE.—This is a body consisting partly of representatives of the University Court and partly of representatives of the Town Council of Edinburgh in which is vested the patronage of certain University chairs which previously were in the gift of the Town Council of Edinburgh. Curators of Patronage

UNIVERSITIES COMMITTEE OF PRIVY COUNCIL.— This Committee was constituted under the Universities Act of 1889. It consists of the President of the Privy Council, State and Legal officials connected with Scotland, and the Chancellor and Rector of each University (if members of the Privy Council). The powers and duties of the Universities Committee have been referred to incidentally in the foregoing memorandum. Such powers and Universities Committee of Privy Council.

duties may be exercised and discharged by any three members of the Committee.

Constituent Colleges. At present there is only one College in the University of Edinburgh, but the possible affiliation of other Colleges with the University is contemplated in the Act of 1889.

Faculties. The faculties are four in number, viz. : Arts, Divinity, Law, and Medicine. Each faculty is presided over by a Dean, who is elected from among the Professors of the faculty, with the approval of the Senate. The science chairs belong, at present, either to the faculty of Arts or to the faculty of Medicine; but there is a committee, consisting of the Science Professors, which deals with all matters immediately connected with science degrees.

Affiliated Colleges: and Recognised Teachers. Extra Academical Teachers, in the Faculty of Medicine, are recognised by the University Court on conditions laid down by the Court. Attendance at the lectures of such teachers is accepted in lieu of attendance at the regular College courses, but in medicine no student can make more than two of the four "medical years" required for a degree by attendance on such courses (regulations now in force). Candidates for a science degree may make two of the three years required for such a degree at a college or school which has been specially recognised for the purpose. Such recognition is accorded only to institutions which are able to satisfy the University Court that they possess the necessary appliances for teaching thoroughly the subject in which recognition is applied for. The teachers must be men of high standing in their profession, and recognition is never given to one individual in more than one subject, except in those cases in which two cognate subjects are taught by one teacher in the University. Extra Academical Teachers have no share in the government of the University, nor have institutions whose teaching is recognised for the purposes of graduation any representation on the Court or the governing bodies of the University.

An association for the purpose of providing short courses of lectures of an academic character for the benefit of persons unable to attend the University itself exists in connection with the University. All Professors of the University are entitled to deliver such courses when willing to do so, but the active staff consists of University graduates other than the Professors. *Extension Lectures.*

Attendance on such lectures is not accepted as forming part of any degree curriculum.

"Local Examinations" are conducted by a University Board on the lines of the Oxford and Cambridge Local Examination Schemes. Certificates are granted in connection with the examinations. *Examination of Intermediate Schools, &c.*

UNIVERSITY CERTIFICATES in Arts are open to competition to *women*, who, after passing the Senior Local examination of one of the Universities, attend at least three of the classes of the Edinburgh Association for the University Education of Women.

TITLES.—M.A.; B.D.; D.D.; LL.B.; B.L.; M.B.; C.M.; M.D.; B.Sc. (in departments of Mathematical, Physical and Natural Sciences, Engineering, Public Health, Agriculture); D.Sc. (in all the branches enumerated except Agriculture), and also in Mental Science and Philology. *Degrees.*

In Arts the pass degree of M.A. is conferred after examination in Latin, Greek, Mathematics, Physics, Mental Science and English Literature. At present there are no alternative courses. *Pass and Honours and Order of Merit.*

The names in the pass list are arranged alphabetically.

HONOURS.—There are four departments for graduation in Arts with honours, in any one of which candidates may present themselves for examination.

The four departments are:—Classical Literature, Philosophy, Mathematics and Physics, Natural Science. There are two grades of honour in the first three departments, each representing a uniform standard. The names in each class are arranged alphabetically.

In the Department of Natural Science there is only one class for honours, in which the names are arranged alphabetically.

There is no honours class in any Department of the Science degree.

Amount of Residence.

RESIDENCE. For the M.A. degree (pass or honours) four winter sessions, of which the last two must be spent at the University of Edinburgh; the others may be passed at any other Scottish University.

For the B.Sc. degree the regulations vary according to the department in which a student intends to graduate. In the departments of Mathematics, Physics, and Natural Science, the term of residence required is three years, two of which may be passed at a college or university recognized for that purpose by the University of Edinburgh.

The number and nature of Examinations for Degrees.

For the M.A., pass degree, there is one examination in each of the three departments of Classics, Mathematics (including Physics), and Philosophy (including English Literature). The examination in the three departments may be taken at different times or together. The examination is conducted partly in writing and partly orally.

For the honours degree there is one examination in each of the departments in which honours are granted.

For the B.Sc. degree in the departments of Mathematics, Physics and Natural Science, there are two examinations. The first examination, which is the same for the three departments of the degree mentioned, includes Mathematics, Physics, Chemistry, Zoology and Botany. The subjects for the second examination are divided into the three groups of Mathematical Sciences, Physical Experimental Sciences, and Natural Sciences. Candidates may select any one of the groups.

D.Sc. Degree. Candidates for this degree must

previously have taken the B.Sc. degree. They are required to pass an examination in one of the sciences, and to submit a thesis containing either an account of original work or historical or critical research connected with the special subject of their examination.

Matriculation Examination. Students are not subjected to any examination as a preliminary to matriculation.

Arts students may omit attendance at the junior classes in Latin and Greek, and may complete the course of study required for the M.A. degree in *three years,* if at the time of entrance to the University they pass an examination in Latin and Greek.

Candidates for the B.Sc. degree are required to pass an examination in general knowledge similar to the Medical Preliminary Examination, before they are admitted to the first B.Sc. Examination.

Other Examinations accepted in lieu of the University Examination. A University Degree, University Local Examination Certificates, &c, exempt from the Preliminary Science Examination in general knowledge. Under no circumstances is exemption from the University degree examinations, or any part of them, granted to candidates.

Provisions for securing high and uniform Standard. Uniformity is secured by the presence of the teachers in the examining board; a high standard by associating external examiners with the teachers.

Provisions for encouraging research and original work. The University has in its gift a large number of scholarships, fellowships, and prizes for students and graduates in Arts and Science. There is a University "Travelling Fund" (the interest of which amounts to about £88 per annum) established for the purpose of assisting graduates of any faculty to travel for the purposes of study or research.

Recent Ordinances of the University Commissioners appointed under the Act of 1889. Preliminary Examination. By ordinances of the University Commissioners which have just been published, students are required, before entering on the curriculum for the M.A. degree, to pass a preliminary examination in (1) English, (2) Latin or Greek, (3) Mathematics, (4) one of the following:—Latin or Greek (if not already taken), French, German, Italian, Dynamics. In future attendance in any class shall not qualify for graduation unless the whole of the preliminary examination has been passed.

M.A. Pass Degree.
Candidates for the ordinary degree of M.A. may follow the curriculum and take the degree in accordance with the scheme hitherto in force, which is described above, provided that they pass the Preliminary Examination, or they may vary their curriculum in the following manner:—Candidates who take the alternative course are required to attend full courses in at least seven subjects, extending over not less than three sessions. Of these subjects four must be (*a*) Latin or Greek; (*b*) English, or a Modern Language, or History; (*c*) Logic and Metaphysics or Moral Philosophy; (*d*) Mathematics or Natural Philosophy. The remaining subjects may be selected from a list of 27 subjects grouped under the four departments of (1) Language and Literature, (2) Mental Philosophy, (3) Science, (4) History and Law; but the whole subjects taken must include either (*a*) both Latin and Greek, or (*b*) both Logic and Moral Philosophy, or (*c*) any two of the following three subjects:— Mathematics, Natural Philosophy, Chemistry.

M.A. Honours Degree.
Candidates for honours must attend 7 classes, taking at least two classes in each of their honours subjects.

Candidates may be examined in the subjects not included amongst their honours subjects at any time during their curriculum; but the whole examination in a candidate's Honours group must be taken at one time.

Science Degree.
The principal alterations made in the regulation for science degrees are as follows:—The Entrance Examination prescribed for the M.A. degree is substituted for the preliminary examination, but science candidates are allowed to take French or German instead of Latin or Greek, and are required to pass Mathematics in a higher standard than is required for the M.A. degree.

The arrangement of a first and second examination is maintained, but in the second examination the subjects are not grouped as heretofore, candidates being allowed to select any three sciences from a list of nine. Candidates must attend seven courses of instruction, spread over a period of not less than three academical years.

A distinction is drawn between degrees in Pure and Applied Science; the ordinance contains regulations for the former only, but states that degrees in Applied Science may hereafter be instituted by special Ordinances of the Commissioners, or after the expiring of their powers by the University Court in each University. [J. J. DOBBIE.]

University of Edinburgh.
NOTE AS TO FINANCE.

Statement of Capital of the University in 1889, and of Income and Expenditure for 1888-89.

Sources of Revenue.
The University is maintained—1. By interest, &c., accruing from Capital Funds in charge of the Senatus Academicus; 2. By the proceeds of a Fund in charge of the University Court; 3. By annual payment made from Crown and Parliamentary grants, and from an annuity payable by Act of Parliament out of the Revenues of the Harbour and Docks of Leith; 4. By Matriculation, Graduation, and other Fees, paid annually; and 5. By annual payments by public bodies or private persons, and from Bursary Funds, of which neither principal nor interest is in the hands of the Senatus. The amount of income derived from the last of these sources is not known with certainty, but is believed to amount to upwards of £1,600 annually.

NOTE.—By the Universities (Scotland) Act of 1889, the whole of the University property formerly vested in the Senatus Academicus is now vested in the Court.

A. Capital in charge of the Senatus Academicus, including floating balances, as at 31st August, 1889.
  I. Destined for special purpose, by deed, statute, or ordinance.

	£	s.	d.
1. Salaries of Professors...	92,470	19	9
2. Class expenses and assistants......	11,848	12	4
3. Bursaries, scholarships, fellowships, and prizes	239,752	12	8
4. For bursaries and prizes entrusted to individual members of Senate and others ...	12,220	1	6
5. Miscellaneous	15,068	1	10

II. Capital, the income of which is applicable for the general purposes of the University (chiefly derived from bequests) ... £40,874 7 8.
III. Disposable capital belonging to General University Fund, as at 31st August, 1889 ... 29,249 14 11

Total capital in charge of Senate previous to the passing of the Act of 1889 (now vested in University Court) ... £441,484 10 8

B. Capital vested in the University Court for further endowment of the Chairs in the Faculty of Arts ... 17,961 4 3

C. Income of the University, destined by Deed, Statute, or Ordinance.
1. Salaries of Professors (derived from interest of funds in hands of Senate, see A 1) from Leith Harbour Annuity, Parliamentary Grants, Deanery of Chapel Royal, Land Revenues of Crown, Income from funds *not* vested in University authorities) ... 10,927 7 7
2. Class assistants and class expenses (from the General University Fund, and other sources) 1,600 3 2
3. Special Parliamentary Grant for Non-Professorial Examiners... 540 0 0
4. For Scholarships, Bursaries, and Prizes (chiefly from Capital Fund in hands of Senate) ... 8,944 10 7
5. For Miscellaneous purposes specified, including £763. 16s. 0d. for Gifford Lectureship ... 1,676 10 4

Total Destined Income ... £23,688 11 8

D. Total University Income.
1. Destined Income as above ... £23,688 11 8
2. Income from General Fund, less amount destined by Ordinance for Assistants and Class Expenses ... 15,569 16 2

£39,258 7 10

E. Income and Expenditure of General University Fund 1888-89,
I. INCOME. £ s. d.
1. Matriculation Fees ... 3,479 10 0
2. Graduation Fees... 7,698 17 6
3. Fees of Registration of Members of General Council... 324 0 0
4. Fees of admission to Library ... 63 10 6
5. Compensation for Stationers' Hall Privileges relinquished, for two years... 1,150 0 0
6. Grant from Government to aid in maintaining and repairing buildings ... 500 0 0
7. Interest of invested Funds (see A III.) ... 911 14 2
8. From Funds bequeathed to the University for general purposes ... 730 5 6

9. Funds partly appropriated to special purposes, the surplus revenues of which fall to the General University Fund ... 1,359 8 6
10. Miscellaneous Receipts ... 87 10 0

£16,304 16 2

II. EXPENDITURE.

I. University Court.   £ s. d.   £ s. d.
  1. Secretary's Salary... 102 7 4
  2. Printing, Advertising ... 67 2 7
  3. Stationery and Incidental ... 16 14 5   186 4 4

II. Senatus Academicus.
  1. Secretary's Salary... 243 15 0
  2. Clerk's ,, ... 221 16 2
  3. Assistant Clerks' Salary ... 195 0 0
  4. Dean of Faculty of Medicine 97 10 0
  5. Dean of Faculty of Art's salary ... 73 2 8
  6. Dean of Faculty of Divinity's salary ... 29 5 0
  7. Dean of Faculty of Law's salary 48 15 0
  8. Incidental Expenses ... 251 5 2
               1,160 9 0

III. University General Council.
  1. Secretary's salary ... 9 15 0
  2. Fees to Registrar and Assistants ... 128 2 0
  3. Meetings, Advertisements ... 43 3 3
               181 0 3

IV. Management, Including Law Agent's Account   382 12 7
V. Editing Calendar ...   29 5 0
VI. Library ...   2,243 1 6
VII. Museums and Teaching Appliances   403 10 0
VIII. Buildings, Maintenance, Repairs, Heating, Lighting, Public Burdens, &c. ...   4,903 11 9
IX. Service ...   908 19 11
X. Class Assistants and Class Expenses ...   2,314 0 0
XI. Examiners ...   1,028 14 0
XII. Printing and Advertising ...   446 9 11
XIII. Class Medals and Prizes...   274 5 0
XIV. Graduation Expenses ...   93 4 0
XV. Incidental Grants, chiefly to Students' Societies ...   588 6 6

Total General Fund Expenditure ... £15,143 13 9
Surplus of Revenue ... 1,161 2 5

Leaving Income ... £16,304 16 2

SALARIES OF ADDITIONAL EXAMINERS FOR DEGREES
(*i.e.*, Examiners in addition to the Professors).

Classical Literature	£120 0 0
Mental Philosophy	120 0 0
Mathematics	120 0 0
Schoolmaster's Diploma	3 3 0
Medicine—13 Examiners at £75	975 0 0
Divinity—2 Examiners at £26. 5s.	52 10 0
Law—2 Examiners at £26. 5s.	52 10 0
Civil Engineering	3 3 0
Agriculture—4 Examiners at £3. 3s.	12 12 0
	£1,458 18 0

NOTE.—The Examiner in Mathematics and certain of the Examiners in Medicine also examine for Science Degrees.

BURSARY, SCHOLARSHIP AND FELLOWSHIP FUNDS.

The total capital destined for Bursaries, Scholarships and Fellowships amounted in 1889 to £251,972. 14s. 2d. The total income destined for the same purposes amounted to £8,944. 10s. 7d., chiefly interest derived from the above capital.

CLASS FEES.

In the foregoing statement the class fees, which form the greater part of the emolument of most of the Professors, do not appear.

POST-GRADUATE STUDIES : ORIGINAL RESEARCH.

ARTS AND SCIENCE.—In addition to about 80 bursaries open to undergraduates, there exist in connection with the University of Edinburgh, numerous prizes, scholarships and fellowships for the encouragement of original research and advanced study.

Prizes.—The prizes which take the form of medals, books, or money are in some cases confined to graduates, in others open to all matriculated students: thus the Lord Rector's Prize of 25 guineas for the best essay on an historical subject is open to all matriculated students.

Scholarships and Fellowships.—The distinction between scholarships and fellowships is purely arbitrary. They are between 50 and 60 in number, and have been founded by private munificence for the encouragement of special branches of study, including nearly all the subjects taught in the Arts and Science Classes. The smallest scholarship is of the annual value of £20, the highest £121, the average annual value being about £70. The conditions of appointment and tenure are very various. The great majority are open only to graduates (in some cases only to honoursmen), of not more than three or four years' standing, but some are attached to special classes, and others are open to undergraduates who have completed a specified curriculum, other than a degree curriculum. A limit of age is imposed in many cases. Scholars are generally required to reside at the University of Edinburgh, and to follow a prescribed course of study, science graduates in some cases being required to proceed to the degree of D.Sc. (involving original research) during their tenure of a scholarship. The holders of certain scholarships are bound to furnish the Senate from time to time with proof that they are pursuing the course of study or research for the encouragement of which their scholarship was awarded. The conditions of tenure of some of the ordinary scholarships allow the holders to travel. But there has recently been established a special fund for the purpose of assisting graduates of any faculty, of not more than three years' standing, to travel for purposes of study or research. The interest of this fund amounts to about £88 per annum. Grants from it have been made for such various purposes as the following :—To assist a science graduate in carrying on investigations at the marine station at Naples ; to assist a law graduate in studying different forms of judicial procedure in German and other Courts of Law ; to assist an arts graduate in studying philosophy at Heidelberg.

Besides the scholarships here referred to several valuable prizes and scholarships for the encouragement of science exist in connection with the Faculty of Medicine. [J. J. DOBBIE.]

II. University of Aberdeen.

As far as the purposes of this pamphlet are concerned, the constitution and arrangements of the University of Aberdeen are in all essential particulars the same as those of the University of Edinburgh.

III. University of Glasgow.

Summary of Constitution, and of Degree Regulations in Arts and Science, etc.

CONSTITUTION :

The University is governed by the University Court and the Senatus Academicus. The respective functions of these bodies will be seen from the abstract below. *(The Governing Bodies.)*

UNIVERSITY COURT. (a) *Constitution.* The Court consists of (a) the Rector, (b) the Principal, (c) the Lord Provost of Glasgow for the time being, (d) an Assessor nominated by the Chancellor, (e) an Assessor nominated by the Rector, (f) an Assessor nominated by the Lord Provost, Magistrates and Town Council of Glasgow, (g) four Assessors elected by the General Council, (h) four Assessors elected by the Senatus Academicus. [The Rector is elected by the Students; the Chancellor by the General Council] *(University Court.)*

The Court is a corporate body, in which is vested all the property of the University.

(*b*) *Functions.* To administer the whole revenue and property of the University. To review decisions of the Senatus appealed against by any member of the Senatus or other member of the University interested; and to receive representations and reports from the Senatus and General Council. To appoint Professors, Examiners and Lecturers, and to define the limits and scope of their duties.

Senatus Academicus. SENATUS ACADEMICUS. (*a*) *Constitution.* The *Principal* and *Professors* only.

(*b*) *Functions.* The ordinary superintendence and regulation of the teaching and discipline of the University. Appoints two-thirds of all standing Committees charged with the superintendence of University Libraries or Museums; receives reports of all such Committees in the first instance, and, subject to review by the University Court, may confirm, modify, or reject such reports.

General Council. GENERAL COUNCIL. This is a purely deliberative body composed of the Graduates of the University.

The General Councils of the Universities of Glasgow and Aberdeen jointly return one representative to Parliament.

GRADUATION.

Degrees are conferred in the Faculties of Divinity, Arts, Science, Law, and Medicine.

The following is an outline of the regulations in Arts and Science. (See note at end).

ARTS.

Graduation in Arts. The degree of M.A. only is conferred in this faculty. Candidates must pass an Examination in (1) Classics, (2) Mental Philosophy, (including *Pass Examination* English Language and Literature), (3) Mathematical Science (Mathematics and Natural Philosophy).

The qualifying course of study extends over four years, but may be completed in three on passing at entrance a preliminary examination in Latin and in Greek.

Examination for Honours.
Honours of two classes may be taken in any or all of these departments. Certain work is prescribed, and besides work is professed by the Candidates.

The degree of M.A. with Honours (of one class only) may be taken in *Natural Science*. The curriculum in Natural Science is, however, distinct from, *and in addition to*, the ordinary curriculum for the degree of M.A.

SCIENCE.

Graduation in Science.
Two degrees, B.Sc. and D.Sc., are conferred in the Faculty of Science. The degree of B.Sc. is given in (1) Natural Science, (2) Engineering Science.

(1) NATURAL SCIENCE.

Ordinary Degree of B.Sc.
Candidates must pass a First Examination in the following five subjects:—

Mathematics	Chemistry
Natural Philosophy	Botany
	Zoology

Curricula: (a) Natural Science.
and a Second Examination in *One* of the following five groups of subjects:—

I. Mathematics and Natural Philosophy.
II. Experimental Physics and Chemistry.
III. Astronomy, Geology, and Mineralogy.
IV. Botany, Zoology.
V. Physiology, Vertebrate Anatomy.

(2) ENGINEERING SCIENCE.

(b) Engineering Science.
This Department is divided into four alternative courses:—(*a*) Civil Engineering, (*b*) Chemical and Mining Engineering, (*c*) Mechanical and Electrical Engineering, (*d*) Naval Architecture and Marine Engineering.

Graduation
in Science
with Honours.

Degree of
D.Sc.

Candidates may present themselves for a further Examination for Honours in any of the five groups in Natural Science, or in the course selected in Engineering Science.

For the degree of D.Sc., Candidates are eligible if they have taken the degree of B.Sc. with honours, and are graduates of at least five years' standing. They must produce some original work and be prepared to undergo examination, practical or written, or both, in the higher departments of their subjects.

[N.B.—The above regulations for graduation in Arts and Science are modified very materially in the ordinances of the University Commissioners now before Parliament. A synopsis of these changes, which applies equally to Glasgow University, is given in Dr. Dobbie's Memorandum on the University of Edinburgh. Dr. Dobbie's Notes on Scholarships, Fellowships, etc., are, on the whole, applicable also to the University of Glasgow.]

University of Glasgow.

NOTE AS TO FINANCE.

Abstract of Financial Statement, 1889-90.

Income of the University destined by Deed, Statute, or Conveyance.

I. For Salaries of Principal, Professors, and Lecturers.*

	£	s.	d.	£	s.	d.
From Teinds and Endowments under Charters of James VI., Charles I., Charles II.	3,605	12	10			
From Treasury Grant	2,768	6	8			
,, Deanery of Chapel Royal (Chair of Biblical Criticism)	352	13	10			
,, Special Foundations	1,876	16	9			
				8,603	10	1
II. For Non-Professorial Examiners.						
From Parliamentary Grants	480	0	0			
,, General University Fund	301	18	0			
,, Foundations	45	0	0			
				826	18	0

*The entire fees of students attending classes are paid over to the Professors, and (with a few exceptions) form by far the larger part of their salaries.

III. For Class Assistants and Class Expenses.

	£	s.	d.	£	s.	d.
From General University Fund	455	0	0			
„ Parliamentary Grant	650	0	0			
„ Special Foundations	1,482	6	2			
				1,587	6	2

IV. For Retired Professors.

	£	s.	d.
From Parliamentary Grant	3,051	17	6
Total Income destined to Maintenance of Teaching Staff	14,069	11	9

GENERAL UNIVERSITY FUND.
Income and Expenditure.

INCOME.	£	s.	d.	£	s.	d.
1. Balance of Revenue from Teinds	4,153	14	2			
2. Matriculation Fees	2,049	5	0			
3. Graduation and Examination Fees	4,095	6	0			
4. Library Subscriptions	84	10	6			
5. General Council Registration Fees	245	0	0			
6. Government Compensation for Stationer's Hall Privilege (one year and a quarter)	883	15	0			
7. Income of Legacies for Library	61	0	0			
8. Students' Catalogue	7	0	0			
9. Treasury Grant for Maintenance of Buildings	125	0	0			
				11,704	10	8

EXPENDITURE.	£	s.	d.	£	s.	d.
1. University Court and Senate	500	2	2			
2. General Council	320	3	0			
3. Factors, Law Agents, Auditors	557	3	6			
4. Libraries	1,878	9	2			
5. Hunterian Museum	313	0	0			
6. Observatory	226	8	7½			
7. Buildings (Repairs, Lighting, Heating, &c.)	2,054	2	1			
8. Service, Cleaning, and Maintenance of Grounds	1,398	19	6			
9. Class Assistants and Class Expenses	559	12	6			
10. Printing and Advertising	575	8	10			
11. Prizes and Medals	175	6	9			
12. Examiners (Law, Medical, Extra, &c.)	301	18	0			
13. Interest on Loans from Trust not yet disposable	877	10	0			
14. Miscellaneous (Police, Public Burdens, &c., &c.)	702	7	3			
				10,441	0	5½
Surplus				1,263	10	2½

Income of Trust Funds for Bursaries, Scholarships, and Prizes.

		£	s.	d.
1.	From Capital Funds in charge of the University	7,151	16	7
2.	From Estate managed by Balliol College, Oxford	400	0	0
3.	From Funds in hands of Town Council, Merchants' House, and Trustees	5,785	0	0
	Total	£13,336	16	7

[ANDREW GRAY].

IV. University of St. Andrews.

Summary of Constitution, and of Degree Regulations in Arts and Science, etc.

Bodies constituting the University.
As a corporate body the University consists of a Chancellor, Rector, three Principals, Professors, Registered Graduates, and Alumni, and Matriculated Students ; while its government is vested in the University Court.

CHANCELLOR.

Functions of Chancellor.
The Chancellor is elected for life by the General Council of the University, of which he is President. He is the official head of the University. Any change proposed by the University Court must receive his sanction. He is entitled to confer Academical Degrees upon persons found qualified by the Senatus.

Government of the University.
The Government of the University is in the hands of the *University Court* and the *Senatus Academicus.*

UNIVERSITY COURT.

University Court.
The University Court was instituted by the Universities (Scotland) Act, 1858; but its membership was largely increased and its powers were greatly extended by the Universities (Scotland) Act, 1889. As thus reconstituted, the court consists of the following seventeen members :—(*a*) Rector

(elected by the students), (*b*) The Principal of the University, (*c*) The Principal of St. Mary's College, (*d*) The Principal of University College, Dundee, (*e*) An Assessor nominated by the Rector, (*g*) The Provost of St. Andrews, (*h*) The Provost of Dundee, (*i*) Four Assessors elected by the General Council, (*j*) Three Assessors elected by the Senatus Academicus. (*k*) Two representatives of the Council of University College, Dundee.* Seven members of the Court constitute a quorum. The Rector and his Assessor continue in office for three years, but in the event of the Chancellor or Rector ceasing to hold office, his Assessor shall continue to be a member of the University Court until an assessor is nominated by the new Chancellor or Rector, and no longer. The other Assessors continue in office for four years, but all assessors are eligible for re-election.

<small>(a) *Constitution of University Court.*</small>

The University Court is a body corporate, with perpetual succession and a common seal, and in it is vested all the property, hereditable and moveable, formerly belonging to the University College of St. Andrews.

Powers. (1) To review all decisions of the Senatus Academicus, and to be a court of appeal from the Senatus in every case, except as otherwise provided in the Universities Act of 1858.

<small>(b) *Powers of University Court,* under Act of 1858.</small>

(2) To require due attention on the part of the Professors to Regulations as to the mode of teaching, and other duties imposed on the Professors.

(3) To administer and manage the whole revenue and property of the University.

(4) To review any decision of the Senatus Academicus on a matter within competency which may be appealed against by a member of the Senatus, or other member of the University having an interest in the decision.

---

*No representative of the University College, Dundee, may sit and vote in the University Court while any matter concerning the funds and estates at present belonging to the University of St. Andrews, as now existing, is under discussion.

(5) To review on appeal decisions of Senatus Academicus.

(6) To appoint Professors and Examiners, and define duties, etc.

SENATUS ACADEMICUS.

Constitution and Powers of Senatus.
The Senatus Academicus consists of the Principals and Professors of the University,* *which includes the Professors of the University College, Dundee.* It regulates and superintends the teaching and discipline of the University; and appoints two-thirds of the members of any committee or committees charged by the Universities Commissioners with the immediate superintendence of the libraries and museums of the University, or the contents thereof. The Senatus receives in the first instance all reports by such committee or committees, and, subject to the review of the University Court, confirms, modifies, or rejects the recommendations in such reports.

The Senatus elects three Assessors to the University Court; and also a Commissioner to the General Assembly of the Church of Scotland.

GENERAL COUNCIL.

General Council.
A General Council, composed of the body of graduates, exists with exactly the same functions and powers as in the other Scottish Universities.

GRADUATION IN ARTS AND SCIENCE.

Graduation.
The regulations for the degree of M.A. (the only degree conferred in Arts) are precisely similar to those sketched above for Glasgow.

The degree of B.Sc. is conferred in the Departments of Physical and Natural Science, and

---

* There are fifteen Professors in the three Colleges of the University of St. Andrews, nine in University College, Dundee.

Engineering Science. Students of University College, Dundee, are eligible for the degree of B.Sc.

The degree of D.Sc. is conferred on candidates of at least one year's standing as Bachelors of Science who pass a satisfactory higher examination, and produce a thesis of merit embodying some original researches on the subject of examination.

[ANDREW GRAY.]

IRELAND.

I. University of Dublin.

1. **Constituent College**—Trinity College, Dublin.
2. **Government.**
    1. Chancellor appointed by Crown.
    2. Visitors: Vice-Chancellor and Lord Chief Justice of Ireland.
    3. α. *Board.*
        i. Provost (by Crown) 1
        ii. 7 Senior Fellows 7
                                                                8

    The Board has exclusive control over
        i. General Finance of College.
        ii. Divinity School.
        iii. Private Endowments.

    β. *Council.*
        i. Provost 1
        ii. 4 Members elected by Senior Fellows 4
        iii. 4   ,,   ,,   ,, Junior ,,   4
        iv. 4   ,,   ,,   ,, Professors who are not Fellows 4
        v. 4 Members elected by Members of Senate who have no vote under preceding heads 4
                                                     17

The Council has probouleutic powers in questions of studies and appointments to Professorships: the final decision on these matters lies with the Board, which, however, usually accepts the recommendations of the Council.

γ. *Senate.*
All Doctors and Masters of the University who have kept their names on the books.
The Senate is the *University* as distinct from the *College* governing body.
Powers: Granting degrees.
Settling conditions of such grants.

University Legislation.

Additions to Charter are made by *Queen's Letter*, which is an act of the Board and the Visitors.
Alterations of Charter by *New Statute*, which requires an Act of Parliament.

N.B.—The Board may apply for new statutes without consulting the other Bodies.

Research.

Professorships about £200 each.
Studentships: Prizes at Degree Examination, £100 a year for 5 years. (No conditions of work or research.)

Rewards.

From £6,000 to £8,000 a year in various prizes.

Finance.

It is difficult to separate the finance of the University from that of the College.

II. *(a)* Queen's University.

Now defunct.

---

1. **Constituent Colleges**—Belfast, Galway, Cork.
2. **Government** entirely in hands of *University Senate.*

a. *Constitution.*
  i. Chancellor (by Crown) 1
  ii. Presidents of Constituent Colleges ... 3
  iii. Representatives of Academical Staffs. 3
  iv. Nominees of Crown holding office during pleasure 17
  —
  24

The Senate elected from its own number a Vice-Chancellor, who officiated in the Chancellor's absence.

β. *Powers.*
  i. *Administrative.*
   Administer Funds of University, found Scholarships, etc.
  ii. *Academical.*
   Fix qualifying courses of study, regulate Degree Examinations, etc.

N.B. — No University Court. — Convocation of Graduates established later.

3. **Seat of University**—Dublin.

4. **Faculties**—Arts and Science, Law, Medicine.

5. **Qualification for Degree.**
  a. *Ordinary.*—Completion of course of study approved by Senate in one of Queen's Colleges.

(N.B.—*Medical.*—In case of Medical Degree two-thirds of qualifying number of lectures may be taken with teachers recognised by the University Senate, other than those of the Queen's Colleges).

  β. *Extraordinary*—Degrees may by *special grace* be conferred on Graduates of other Universities.

6. **Visitor**—The Crown.

N.B.—The University Senate had no power to interfere in the government of the Queen's Colleges.

II. (b) Royal University of Ireland.

1. Chancellor.
2. Senate.
3. Convocation of *male* graduates.

   Senate.
     30 Appointed by Crown 30
      6 Elected by Convocation 6
                                                      36

All government and administration of University in hands of Chancellor and Senate. Powers of Convocation restricted to right of making representations.

Note as to Finance of Royal University.

1. Administration.

Office	£3,500	
Travelling Expenses—Senate	450	
Stationery, Printing, etc.	500	
Incidental	500	
		£4,950

2. Examinations.

Examiners	£5,000	
Fellows	5,000	
Superintendents	600	
Travelling—Examiners and Superintendents	1,200	
Incidental	250	
		12,050

3. Rewards.

Exhibitions (money prizes)	£2,200	
Scholarships for 3 years	700	
†Studentships, 5 every year of £100 for 3 years	1,300	
		4,200
		£21,200

Income.

Government Grant	£20,000	
Fees	4,000	
Interest on Capital	1,100	
		£25,100

† The total is £1,300 instead of £1,500, owing to a provision of the Charter that if the winner of a Studentship holds or wins a money prize in any State-endowed College, the amount of such prize must be deducted from the Studentship.

Museum Collections, etc.
Government gave... ... ...£5,000
University ,, ... 5,000
————— £10,000

Buildings.
Given by Government, cost roughly ...£100,000

N.B.—Large proportion of expenditure and fee income is connected with Medical Degrees. Medical Fees £1,500.

Exhibitions are money prizes given at every Examination (cf. London).

Scholarships are given at Matriculation, and tenable for three years; but holder must gain honours in each examination subsequent.

Studentships are given at M.A. Examination. No conditions of work or research.

1 in Mathematics.   ⎫
1 ,, Classics.   ⎬ Each year.
1 ,, Mental Science.   ⎭

1 ,, Modern Languages.   ⎫
1 ,, Experimental Science. ⎬ Alternate years.

1 ,, History.   ⎫
1 ,, Biology.   ⎬ Alternate years.

In all Examinations, except Matriculation, candidates are examined orally as well as by paper : and in Science subjects and Music the examinations are largely practical.

[H. R. REICHEL.]

www.ingramcontent.com/pod-product-compliance
Lightning Source LLC
Chambersburg PA
CBHW020257090426
42735CB00009B/1121